RIDE WITH US!

15,642 MILES, 70 NIGHTS CAMPING
Mastered by Bucket List Couple in Their Late 80's

BY **SPORTYMAN**

Ride With Us! 15,642 Miles, Seventy Nights Camping
–Mastered by Bucket List Couple in Their Late 80's.

F I R S T   E D I T I O N
Published in 2025

Written by: James A Staggers |
email: concernedgrandparents361@gmail.com

Paperback ISBN: 978-0-578-69462-7

Library of Congress Case
Staggers, James A.
Ride With Us! 15,642 Miles, Seventy Nights Camping
–Mastered by Bucket List Couple in Their Late 80's.
Case Number: 1-14737160601 | February, 2025

Library of Congress Cataloging-in-Publication Data

Category: Autobiography, Travel, America, Alaska, Road Trip, Bucket List

Cover Designed by: Eli The Book Guy

Formatting by: EliJah & Jahshua Blyden | www.EliTheBookGuy.com

Published & Printed in the USA, Tampa, Florida |
A&A Printing & Publishing | www.PrintShopCentral.com

FORWARD

My intent when chronicling this adventure is to inform readers, who may aspire to make the journey; either by perusal or planning. Preparations commenced four months prior to departure on Saturday, June 8, 2024 and required 80 hours to complete.

Recreational vehicle campgrounds availability has become exceedingly more difficult since the COVID pandemic.

When making phone calls in February, I discovered that many Canadian and Alaskan facilities are not operating at that time of year, and my attempts to contact continued through the month of May. At time of departure eight remain "in limbo", and created an uneasiness for Nancy. Her primary concern is the potential to encounter a grizzly bear. I have assured her that our Class C motorhome will be a safe haven. Nevertheless, she markedly prefers a populated site to boondocking. (camping void of electric and water).

Canadian border restrictions prevent the transport of firearms, thus I purchased a glock imitation CO_2 revolver. It most certainly will not hamper a bear's intention, however it could restrain an unwanted intruder. Previously three weeks had been the extend of our camping history, and ten weeks would no doubt present some challenges.

Family and friends had cautioned us that our relationship might be "in peril" given twenty-four seven in a twenty-two-foot enclosure. I countered that underneath the awning could serve as my doghouse if needed.

We decidedly favor state parks rather than commercial campgrounds: always less expensive and typically more inviting. Most permit campfires and some lake swimming. Canada and Alaska have a very short supply of full hook-up aforesaid offerings. Only twenty-two of the preferred locations were booked for the planned seventy nights. San Diego, California and Yellowstone State Parks were completely occupied, despite my early request; waiting lists were not in vogue.

My primary apprehension is motorhome failures: only that the delay would require altering scheduled reservations. A benefit of retirement is flexibility. Completing the journey before the snow and ice arrive is the only necessity.

Our conveyance is five years in age, with only 25,000 miles and equipped with a generator.

As you will read, the journey was completed without any major interruptions.

Anyone declaring that the excitement of life has concluded by the time age eighty-five "comes a round", has yet to "bag" this adventure.

TABLE OF CONTENTS

DAY #1

Te drive through the Gorge on 1-40 is always seductive. For nearly 30 miles the highway parallels the Pigeon River with solid rock walls on both borders. This landscape, and especially large boulders, imparts an intense sensation of strength to my mental disposition: Not to be confused with power. I sense that I can master any challenge that I encounter. For probably the previous twenty years I have relished this reckoning, and welcome the invitation as we commenced this ten-week bucket list experience. The uplifting "emboldment" generates an eagerness "to see what lies ahead".

The morning commenced at 6:00 a.m. for me and 7:00 a.m. for Nancy. At 9:15 a.m. we finished loading the refrigerated meals and turned the ignition key on at 25,355 miles on the odometer. We were blessed with glorious sunshine and 62 degree weather on June 8, 2024 in Franklin, North Carolina, (about one hour south of Asheville). As we departed our golf course community, we observed only vacant greens: Why no golfers on a beautiful Saturday morning? (Yes, at my advanced age, I do take time to "smell the roses": Which I didn't do as a younger and busier father). The Farmers Market in downtown was lively with tourists and every day residents. (In summer months, half of the license plates are Florida). On the north edge of town we accelerated to 65 miles per hour to climb the 3-mile Cowee Mountain. We commenced our descent at 50 miles per hour: Fully loaded, I was pleased with the horsepower. Since our last outing, we have added a spare tire mechanism to the rear bumper. It seems inconceivable that a rig like ours is manufactured without that "necessity". We are not visiting Alaska void of a spare tire.

Rockslides in the gorge are to be expected, and we had one-lane traffic for 3 miles. Trucks are restricted to the right lane in that area, and traffic moves at about 45 miles per hour: slowing down provides more time to view the landscape and "get strong" for the 2.5 month adventure. We entered Pisgah National Forest, 500,000 acres of hard wood, which also borders my home over an hour distant. We then entered Cherokee National Forest and crossed the Appalachian Trail. Buses with multiple layers of roof top rubber rafts dotting the roadway, attests to the local white water rafting. The next exit is labeled as the entrance to the Smoky Mountain National Park (the most visited National Park in the U.S.). Shortly after crossing the French Broad River (which also borders the Biltmore Mansion in Asheville), our voyage came to a halt for road construction. Gridlock continued for 45 minutes, and we arrived at Norris Dam State Park in Tennessee near Rocky Top (as made famous by the song) at 1:30 p.m. Then the disappointment emerged; the signage on Route # 441 for the park was comfortably visible. However, signage to locate our campsite didn't exist. Eventually we discovered a Visitors Center, only to receive directions to the west campground after identifying our site as the east campground. The driving terrain was mountainous and narrow, hairpin curves, to both campgrounds: not advisable for the faint of heart. We crossed the dam erected in 1936, the year my parents took their marriage vows, and had a perfect view of an eye-appealing marina on the lake. Vacationers were diving off the pontoon boats into the blue water. The two campgrounds are each 3-5 mile distant from the park entrance. We found our site one hour later and were shocked to see a back-in gravel driveway ending in an unblocked cliff. My loving partner was adamant that we should not reside on that perilous precipice. I called the reservations center and was able, fortunately, to relocate. However, this gravel driveway was unstable to walk on and could easily result in a sprained ankle or worse. The fire ring and picnic table were ten yards from the motorhome location: not user friendly. I transport my own fire pit and table just for this situation, and was able to set-up for the evening in reasonable comfort. We charcoal grilled salmon while observing the wood burning flames. We drove 172 miles today and "all in all" not a bad day, no serious occurrences of consequence.

DAY #2

Nancy slept late on Sunday morning, she then prepared omelets while I had been writing for 2 hours since 6:30 a.m., while enjoying the outside ambience.

We pulled out at 10:20 a.m. for a 3-and-a-half-hour drive, another planned short driving day as training for endurance in the coming days. Beautiful mountains with 74-degree cloudy skies made for a pleasant morning drive. Buc-ee's Service Station in Richmond, Kentucky was a shocking observation with traffic lines completely filling the exit lane and hundreds of vehicles observed in the parking lot. That company has obviously instituted a marketing jewel.

We munched on an Ingle's cinnamon chocolate chip muffin for lunch in the motorhome when fueling up.

Our reservation at Big Bone Lick State Park in Union, Kentucky blossomed absolute joy. It is a national natural landmark: noted for Pleistocene bone beds. The site is recognized as the birthplace of American Vertebrate Paleontology. The Visitor Center displayed fossilized bones and artifacts from the past 18,000 years. We were amazed at the large size of the bones on display. The park also maintains a small herd of bison to commemorate the past. Bison display a hump on their back, and buffalo do not. I was surprised to learn they can jump over a 6-foot hurdle. We dined on "gourmet" hot dogs cooked *over* wood burning coals. We drove 223 miles today - a most enjoyable day.

ᗪᗩY #ᣮ

Being that Cincinnati, Ohio is only twenty miles distant on our route, we departed the campground at 5:40 a.m. in an effort to escape the morning rush hour. We were successful as the by-pass was void of gridlock. (I consider reduced speeds under 40 miles per hour as gridlock). Nancy was disappointed to not be able to see the city, as she has never visited the sister city of Pittsburgh on the Ohio River. We did cross that body of water during the early morning hour. We observed multiple large manicured horse farms when leaving the campground. (Horses have always provided, since as a child asking for a pony, a delight to my sensitivities).

The Indianapolis beltway was not as welcoming. South bound (shortest route) was closed and north bound was congested with closed lanes due to large scale construction. Gusty strong winds required total focus to maintain control as passing Semi's created an unwelcomed draft. What followed was a mostly boring drive looking at young corn and soybean plants. We swapped points in our uniquely devised mind game. Having been raised on a dairy farm, Nancy was unable to distinguish the difference:

She insisted that the corn plants were too close together to be corn, and I insisted that the plants were too tall for soybeans. I was unable to find a farmer walking on the interstate to settle our differences: Thus, we negotiated a stalemate in our game. No points awarded, as when she discerns that I have made a blunder, like not locking a door; she gets a point and vice-versa.

We did sight our first windmill farm on this drive, and they are always an impressive experience. I wonder just how much revenue they provide for the farmers.

Our electric power was lost during the night, and not due to inclement weather.

Adapting to these unexpected experiences maintains our energetic minds as our physical capabilities deteriorate. My two stainless steel knees do limit my flexibility and the A-Fib detracts from my endurance. Nancy has a very slight stability issue, and I constantly assist in transferring our meals in and out of the motorhome.

We feasted on charcoal grilled salmon, and relaxed with another campfire at Jubilee College State Park in Brimfield, Illinois. We rated the campsite as poor, and we drove 383 miles today.

5:25 a.m. Central Time brought beautiful clear skies. We were pleased to see the Propane gauge at two-thirds full, and the freezer food healthy.

We crossed Spoon River before the mighty Mississippi and then in to Iowa. The "World's Largest Truck Stop", identified as Iowa 90 was a startling sight on an otherwise humdrum landscape. Windmills are idle at this point in time. Thirty miles east of Des Moines, we cross the Skunk River. Our first rain was a short shower of ten minutes. As the weather front emerged, the winds arrived and it was necessary to reduce our speed from 70 miles per hour to 60 miles per hour as the young corn plants of two feet were bent to the East. The road surface was very rough making for an uncomfortable ride in the head wind.

Iowa ranks first in the United States in corn production, and is evidenced when observing the landscape. A record was set in 2016 with 2.7 billion bushels harvested.

The State Park, Prairie Rose, in Harlan, Iowa was rated as good, and we drove 352 miles today.

DAY #5

W e left at 5:45 a.m. as our campground for the next two nights is first come-first serve. Buffalo Bill Ranch sounds interesting enough to rest and be a tourist for a day.

Tree branches are not moving this morning and the early sun to our left as we return to Interstate 80 is energizing. Now westbound with the sun in our rearview mirror, I am surprised to see the windmill farm creating power.

Crossing Honey Creek reminds me to appreciate my honey for being my note taking "honey of a traveling secretary".

I just observed a "Ski Area" sign in this flat plain?

We crossed the Missouri River into Nebraska at 6:45 a.m. and encountered minor rush hour gridlock on the Omaha Bypass I-680. Twice in the next hour, we observed an old clunker vehicle towing two more vehicles without license plates. It was the first time in my million plus miles of driving that I have had that experience: It must be legal in Nebraska. Shortly thereafter, we passed a small Fire Department truck with a message on the back: "Keep back 343 feet"? Intended or not, that elicited two chuckles from our 22 foot "home away from home".

The weather forecast for our departed campground was severe storms with tornado warnings. At 8:20 a.m. our speed was reduced to 60 miles per hour as very strong winds commenced buffeting our vehicle. A message lit up my dash stating: "Service Stabili-

Trak" ...I didn't know I had one and don't know what service is required.

A wall of dust was now crossing I-80, and it is my first "dust storm" experience. Fortunately, visibility remained satisfactory.

When we stopped for vehicle fuel ($132.14), I had difficulty standing without swaying. All the grazing cattle were standing gathered in bunches. I wouldn't want to live in this environment. A sign on the highway reads: "Watch for wind on bridges". A temporary sign should read: "All vehicles maximum speed 50 miles per hour".

I am now sitting on the Platte River in the campground watching kayakers while sipping scotch. It is well deserved after two hours of driving with 110% diligence to the steering wheel.

My phone alerted me to thunderstorms and a tornado watch at this location for tomorrow night. I think we will change our plans and leave here tomorrow. I would like to attend a horse show tomorrow morning in our host city of North Platte. We drove by the arena today and viewed hundreds of local ranchers' horses: my kind of preferred surroundings.

This evening, my phone is warning drivers of the I-80 dust storm.

By the way, our disputed game score has Nancy ahead by 15-10. However, remember she is the scorekeeper. The temperature reached 101 degrees this evening. We ventured to an Italian restaurant and had a mediocre meal, after driving 368 miles.

DAY #6

North Platte, Nebraska was hosting the Nebraska Lands Rodeo. Our campground was close enough to hear the public address announcer until 11:00 p.m. last night. I hoped to view the horse arena this morning thus we didn't leave the campground until 7:45 a.m.

Still in the motorhome and on the 2-lane entrance road, we received an unexpected pleasure as we approached the arena rodeo grounds: *A* few dozen cowboys and slim trim young women wearing western apparel were warming up their horses before taking their turn in the arena. So much horse flesh to gaze upon: powerful yet sleek and fast. (Reminded me of my softball tournaments as many players sprinted to the outfield prior to game time to loosen their leg muscles in an attempt to prevent injury.) Nancy was able to capture a few photos of the human and non-human contestants. There were hundreds of horses tied to their trailers and awaiting their call to perform.

We departed town at 8:35 a.m. and drove comfortably until 10:15 a.m. High winds attacked us once more but only for fifteen minutes. The warning alert did not grace my odometer screen: Thank You!

At 12 noon, we entered the West (my declaration) and gave a "Whoop Whoop Horray" as we gladly spied the "Entering Wyoming" welcome sign. We had seen enough corn and soybeans for now. The speed limit in Wyoming is 80 miles per hour, and the

Semi-Trucks whizzed by us constantly. We saw the cattle drinking in Lodge Pole Creek as we traveled North on I -25. We spotted a "Missile Alert Facility" sign, and pondered why it would be located in this remote area. Why would a missile be targeted in cowboy country?

Our westerly driving has changed to north bound for the next 1,300 miles. It was nice to have the sun at our rear every morning. We passed by the community of Chugwater and a Billboard advertising "Stampede Restaurant". The local Creek of the same name was void of water. We then passed signage for "Oregon Trail Ruts", "Cottonwood Creek" and "Horseshoe Creek".

We exited I-25 at Glendo, Wyoming for two nights of planned relaxation: Population 237. I entered a Cowboy bar to ask directions to the State Park as signage didn't exist. WOW! Was my reaction: gorgeous ambience: all western motif: taxidermy of multi species: guns and holsters, and old West memorabilia. I complimented the Owner and headed down the road to the State operated campground at 1:30 p.m. The entrance was operated by a young woman and young man, both in their early twenties. They provided a map but were unable to reserve campsites. They advised reservations can only be made through a national call center. (I have always found this process unsatisfactory, as that source has zero knowledge of the campground). My $16.95 "RV Camping in State Parks" publication states there are 7 campgrounds and 415 sites on the North Platte River with swimming. Previewing many sites to choose a preferred one for two nights was, I deemed, the best decision.

Warning signs declared "Open Range, Loose Livestock". Nancy took pictures of the cattle crossing the isolated road as we halted our progress to heed their grazing choice. We saw our first Pronghorn who stared us down before continuing to search for a desirable meal.

We decided to evaluate the "Sandy Beach" campground as it listed both water and electric hookups and an attractive location. Now the disappointment commenced as we traveled 18 miles on very narrow, steep winding roads. It was necessary to use manual mode on the transmission, as it was impossible to gather speed to climb that elevation change. The signage was sparse and several times we were unsure if we were on the proper route, and twice we discovered that we were not. We finally encountered a maintenance truck and asked the driver for directions. To our dismay, he informed us that we had already passed "Sandy Beach" and that it was not marked. After backtracking to the campsites labeled as "Dunes", I phoned the central reservations number and endured frustration for 45 minutes. The customer rep insisted that an available site was in a location I could not find. The cost was $52 for electric service only. I reached my frustration breaking point and told him "I give up". When leaving the camping area, we saw site #1417 at the opposite end of the circle from site #1418. Apparently, despite his disagreement, his satellite imagery was not nearly as accurate as my physical "walk around". We drove 30 miles and camped at a KOA for $58 with full hook-up.

The Douglas, Wyoming location is home of the "Jackalope" and Wyoming State Fair and Rodeo. This mythical animal is a jackrabbit with antelope antlers. My research revealed that, in actuality, a jack rabbit that has been afflicted with a rare virus does generate clumps that resemble dreadlocks referenced as horns.

Entering a campground for the first time is like a "box of chocolates" as Forrest Gump described: "You never know what you are going to get". I rate each campsite as poor, good or excellent. Glendo State Park in Wyoming received a poor. The KOA received a good: Campsites very close to each other on gravel surface with no view. Swimming pool and community fire pit were available. We drove 413 miles today.

DAY #7

We planned a 3-hour driving day and departed at 10:45 a.m., which afforded me two hours of writing time prior to departure. The skies were heavily overcast as we crossed Box Elder Creek, Hat Six Road and Zero Road in Casper, Wyoming. We were following the Sand

Creek Massacre Trail where the Cheyenne and Arapaho Native Americans lost around 230 of their group who were murdered by American Soldiers. This tragic event took place in 1864.

It was disappointing to again read the "Service StabiliTrak" warning on my dash board. The cross winds were very strong, and the Semi-Trucks traveling in the opposite direction on the 2-lane Highway #26 generated a precarious draft. This undesirable situation persisted for 2 hours. After passing "Hells Half Acre" residence, we spotted another Pronghorn grazing by the roadside. The highway is periodically adorned on either side with cowboy sculptures. We passed through Highland with a population of 4. We witnessed our second dangerous driver when a Pick-Up truck passed our vehicle and a gasoline tanker who had to quickly apply the brakes and swerve to permit the Pick-Up truck's re-entry to the right hand traffic lane. The line of traffic was six vehicles, and he managed to pass two. Where did he think he could go? It was just the kind of ignorant decisions that create accidents and injury or death.

Twenty minutes later, a car sitting on the shoulder pulled out into our lane causing me to immediately apply the brakes as well as my horn. Why didn't the driver see a motorhome? It was a scary experience with a third dangerous driver.

We arrived in Shoshoni (population 471) at 12:45 p.m., our target city for Boyson State Park, crossing our fingers we wouldn't duplicate our sad experience as in Glendo, Wyoming. Signage took us north, and we quickly viewed a sign stating we had entered the Park but there was no visible evidence of a State Park, except the sign. Eight miles later, we were relieved to finally see a campground sign. The entrance was managed by a very congenial and knowledgeable senior lady. She provided a map of available sites and suggested we look at them and pick our preferred site-exactly what should have occurred in Glendo. We camped on a sand site with a private beach entry to the beautiful water on a reservoir. We built a campfire in my portable pit and roasted hot dogs on the beach. It was an absolutely pristine camping experience despite boon docking - probably the best we will find on the entire venture. We were delighted to find an eight-foot-long piece of driftwood and attached it to our rear bumper.

I am hoping the Canadian Border Inspectors will be amenable, as the souvenir trophy will compliment my bank adornments at my North Carolina residence. The landscape has already unveiled Arizona rocks.

We observed our fourth unsafe driver of the journey, and third of the day, as a driver passed us at high speed while my left turn signal was flashing. It was necessary to forcefully apply the brakes to prevent an accident. We drove 160 miles today.

DAY #8

W e crossed Bad water Creek and, as I was making a left hand turn in to a gas station to purchase coffee (with turn signal blinking), a very dangerous driver #5 passed me on the left in the opposing traffic lane.

Fifteen minutes hence, we were surprised to enjoy the sighting of an abundance of snow on the distant mountain range peaks: Snow in the middle of June, WOW! Our first sight of Wind River was accompanied by a very picturesque and interesting cloud formation in the sky. Crossing Bull Lake Creek led us to our first view on the trip of red rocks (iron content), and a sign alerting us to Big Horn Sheep sightings. Unfortunately, we did not discover their presence.

The Wind River crisscrosses our path continuously and as we left the Indian Reservation, we saw military tanks on our left at the Military Museum. The Route #26 West signs took us by "Wind River Painted Rocks", and signs warning "Do Not Approach Bears On The Road". At Togwotee Pass in the Teton National Forest, we topped a mountain and were in awe as the Teton Mountain spirals were covered with snow and just majestic. The dashboard recorded 59 degrees and the elevation was 9,567 feet. I highly advocate the drive we just completed on Route #26, as the landscape is continuously breathtaking. As we entered Yellowstone National Park at 12:00 p.m. with our "forever" park passes, we saw the Snake River in a gorge far below. A visit to the Visitors Center yielded a map of Yellowstone highlights. We stood in line to register at the Grant Village campground for the night. Despite having previously made a reservation and paid, we stood in line for 20 minutes. Their computer had us to arrive the day prior, and the registering clerk changed our reservation to today. As we approached our assigned site, we found two Pick-Up trucks parked in our location. The campground was crowded even more severely than KOA's. We asked questions of campers in order to locate the Pick- U p's owners. When located, they were unapologetic but did remove their vehicles. The site was horrible and congested. We locked ourselves in for the remainder of the day. I had planned to cook over a campfire but abandoned that pleasure. No services, no view, and vehicles passing within 6 feet of our motorhome: "Box of chocolates".

One-tenth of our "bucket list" adventure has elapsed. We are looking forward to our Yellowstone views while driving tomorrow morning.

We drove 217 miles today.

DAY #9

~SUNDAY, JUNE 16TH (FATHER'S DAY)

Since we turned in before dark last night, we woke up early at 5:50 a.m. Mountain Time to bright sunshine and a temperature of 37 degrees. After leaving Grant Village campground, we traversed around Yellowstone Lake with constant views of steam erupting from the soil, and small geysers dotting the landscape. This is the fourth visit to Yellowstone in my lifetime, the first of which was with my parents as a ten-year-old, and this geothermal phenomenon is always a marvel! I remember my awakened realization of how different our world can astonish us when we leave our nesting cocoon. We continued our trek northward past "Old Faithful" (we didn't stop as both of us have witnessed the eruption) to Biscuit Basin. The highway borders Madison River, followed by Gibbon River and the falls of the same name. We ventured on to Roaring Mountain to view a unique wonder of nature. The mountain is white as the multiple geysers generate sulfide gases, which forms sulfuric acid when reacting to water vapor and leaches the soil. It is the home of billions of Thermophiles, a microorganism that thrives and reproduces at extremely high temperatures. It is an awesome sight to behold. We then backtracked south for 8 miles to travel east and connect with the eastern loop in Yellowstone, a route that I never traveled previously. We viewed the "Grand Canyon of the Yellowstone" on the Yellowstone River. The waterfall is magnificent! While climbing Mount Washburn (elevation 10,243 feet), we were stopped by a flagman and one-way traffic. As we progressed, a tragic scene appeared. Two vehicles had collided on the narrow and very bendy road and dropped in to a shallow ravine. The Bronco and Pick-Up truck were being excavated by a tow truck utilizing a winch. Had they dropped over the other side of the highway (no guardrails on either side), they would have found their way to the bottom of the mountain. The accident must have occurred much earlier as an ambulance was not present. This was our sixth dangerous driver and first observed accident.

We were surprised to see copious drifts of snow where the sun fails to connect with the earth still existing in June.

We crossed Antelope Creek after our exciting descent from the mountaintop. The hairpin curves on the steep slope were exhilarating as unexaggerated: not recommended for the "faint of heart". We departed Yellowstone at 12:00 p.m. as Nancy took a photo of the famous Northern Entrance Arch. At the same moment, we entered the small cowboy town of Gardiner, Montana. It was a very western scene, and tourists were frequenting the Sunday afternoon bar with live music.

We had hoped, as all visitors do, to see wild life during our 5.2-hour and 126-mile drive, and we were not disappointed. We spied Bison no fewer than eight times; sometimes, large herds, small herds, or solitary and lonely appearing massive animals. Why would one choose to roam alone and not prefer the company of others? One was moseying along the highway and was within two feet of our motorhome as we slowed to examine and photograph. He had a second layer of partial hide on his back. One herd included two mothers with their calves trailing very nearby.

Many times, we saw Pronghorns grazing peacefully.

Shortly before exiting, we were delighted to come upon a large herd of Elk We had to turn the vehicle around twice to get a good lasting view, as there wasn't a pull-off available at that point in the highway.

We drove an additional 84 miles to Bozeman, Montana to buy groceries, tarp and a rope at Wal-Mart. This was our first major grocery shopping since leaving home.

The tarp and rope were to cover the "precious" artifact secured on the back bumper. We were seriously hoping the disguise would be successful when crossing the Canadian border. Cloaked it would appear as additional luggage on a limited luggage vacation home: Fingers crossed!

We subsequently crossed Bridger Mountain Range, Bear Canyon Road and Madison River before arriving at our campground, Lewis and Clark

Caverns. The State Park's book described the location to be on the Jefferson River, and we were disappointed to find the highway and railroad tracks were between the river and the campground. Our site, as were all, was in an open flat valley. There were no nature-developed trees, only planted vegetation. We did have a good view of grassy covered mountains on both sides of the campground. The land was mowed with picnic tables and electric but there were no water or sewer hook-ups. We filled our fresh water tank for a two night planned rest. I expected to build a campfire and cook out for dinner, however the wind was blowing so viscously even the chairs would not remain upright. Thus, Nancy prepared her minestrone soup inside. Fortunately, we had electric service as the heater needed to be employed that night for our comfort. Nancy did not sleep well but I was very comfortable under the covers.

We traveled 264 miles today.

DAY #10

We woke up to threatening skies and soon commenced a rain shower. We hoped to prepare breakfast outside but again no campfire. At least the wind had stopped blowing. The internet was not available on my phone but I was able to see a snow forecast in Montana. We will need to listen to the radio to determine if our travel plans are in jeopardy.

I wrote for two hours while Nancy enjoyed her early morning under the covers. Our heater runs as the thermostat dictates but I added my sleeping blanket to her for comfort. I watched other campers walking their dogs in the light rain.

While conversing with the campground host couple, I learned that it was snowing in the pass at the mountaintop near Butte and icy roads were forecasted for that night and the morning. Is it really the middle of June? What happened to Global Warming?

Nancy and I labored for 1.5 hours tarping and roping our prized possession to the back bumper; nearly every inch must be secured to prevent the tarp from ripping in the wind. We decided to retain our campfire wood and permit the Canadian Inspector at the Border to search for it if he desires. The campground clerical management issued us a $39 refund for a one-night reservation. We departed our site at 1:10 p.m. with an anticipated six-hour drive to the next reserved campground (Eight Flags in Milk River, Alberta, Canada). Arriving at 7:00 p.m. is not our cup of tea but it was preferable to driving through the mountain in treacherous weather conditions. It was 50 degrees in the valley, and the sun was lighting our way.

As we crossed Tobacco Root Mountain, the dash board screen displayed a temperature of 37 degrees, and we encountered a soft rain at 2:00 p.m. Fifteen minutes later at the Sheep Head viewing area signage, the rain began hitting the windshield with solid content and the temperature dropped to 35 degrees.

Sleet changed to snowflakes and, soon thereafter, to a blizzard. Visibility was maintained, as the precipitation was not sticking to the warmer ground surface. However, the wet road surface required diligent maneuvering as our descent progressed at 45 miles per hour. At Bear Gulch, the rain once again appeared and ceased when we crossed Boulder River, In Elkhorn Mountains, the rain stopped briefly and then reappeared at "Gates of the Mountains". At 4:10 p.m., "Little Prickly Bear Creek" revealed stunning rock formations on both sides of the highway. The light rain was intermittent, and the Wolf Creek area necessitated slow progress again as road resurfacing called for one-lane traffic and 50 miles per hour speeds on the constant bends that followed the river. No doubt the early settlers followed the same river through these ravines during their search for Oregon. The "Big Belt Mountains" and the "Sticky Creek" area again presented absolutely gorgeous views which makes the miles "go faster" as the landscape takes precedence with the travelers' preoccupation.

This is why traveling is most enjoyable; just being in the moment and "smelling the roses". Criss crossing the Missouri River numerous times overcame the memory of the boring drive in the Kansas cornfields. The Sun River appeared at "Great Falls Mountain", and we chuckled at the signage at Exit #313 on I-15, which read "Dutton". John and Beth (from the Yel-

lowstone television series) were obviously not residing in this small Montana community, although the
many ravines we traversed today would easily hide
the corpses that John found necessary to discard.

The landscape totally changed to a plateau of
straight highway and permitted 70 mile per hour progress in the 80 mile per hour speed limit permitted area. The farms (the houses were too small to be ranch-
es) were separated by miles. The acreage being cultivated by each of them could easily be 1,000 or even
2,000. Most were producing very short and rich appearing green plants. Perhaps we were looking at lentils as Montana yields 63.4 million pounds a year as
the fourth largest product produced in the State following wheat, hay, barley and peas coming in at #5.
With such vast acreage, we wondered where the main
power and equipment resided to operate the production. The small farm residences and barns did not reveal the answer; however, the storage silos did provide evidence. A modest farm house with six silos
was not unusual. Eventually, we did pass by an
equipment supplier with a large inventory of huge size
vehicles to work the soil. The cost of those machines
was a non-compute as to the small size residences.
It appears all the revenue is utilized for equipment,
and houses and living environments are not personal
priorities. Absolute dedication to crop production was
pictured from the highway. A void of recreational in-
terests like baseball and tennis were in sharp contrast
to the countryside's of our Eastern United States.

We were eventually relieved to see the road sign indication that the "Sweetgrass" Border Crossing was only 34 miles away, and we were happy cam pers! This tenth day of travel is the first day I have become tired of driving. It has been twelve hours since I sipped my morning coffee. Nancy was excited to spot a solitary Elk grazing. Small pumping wells seventeen miles south of the Border were the first we have seen in 3,000 miles. A distinct odor, much like sulfur, permeated the air but we were not able to recognize the source.

As we approached the Border Security at 7:00 p.m., both of us were feeling intense anticipation. I placed my Marine Corps hat on my head, and the Handicap placard on the rearview mirror. A search of our firewood and bumper tarp could easily produce a long delay in our already long day. We were shocked to discover that we were the only vehicle crossing Border, and only one of six lanes was open. The young man in the enclosed small building was surprisingly welcoming and asked: "How has your day been?" His revolver was in plain sight, and I responded: "Very long. How far is Milk River?" At his request, we handed him our Passports and Driver Licenses. "Only ten minutes" was his reply. "How long will you be in Canada?" "Just passing through on our way to Alaska". Any firearms or drugs?" "Only a C02 pistol, no firearms". "How far is its range?" "I don't know." "Have safe travels." I slowly exited his inspection lane, took off my hat and Nancy and I stared at each other in disbelief. There were no sniffing dogs, no vehicle walk-a round, and no questions regarding firewood. The inspection was unbelievably quick and hassle-free. "Hooray-Hooray", we exclaimed, and we only have 3 more Border Crossings on this adventure.

Once again, the campground was a disappointment, even though the "Mile Post Travel Planner" did state that "Eight Flags" is municipally owned. That was a non-compute, as it appeared that all the RV's in this park are full-time residents and most are old and many in shabbiness. Our next-door neighbor had a clothesline and drying garments were prominently displayed within our view. The River and Golf Course are situated directly behind the campground but not in the immediate campsite environment.

Nancy served her tasty homemade chili, and I was in bed at 9:00 p.m. At my request, Nancy woke me up at 10:00 p.m., and I wrote and read until 12:30a.m. I thought that perhaps I might golf tomorrow as our reservations were for two nights.

The literature description is: "The 8 Flags flying over the campground represent 7 governments, including the Hudson Bay Company, all of which laid claim to the Milk River area. Texts to my children, Michelle and Randy, were unsuccessful as there was no Internet.

We drove 325 miles today.

DAY #11

By 5:15 a.m., I had enough sleep and my addictive morning coffee was refreshing. Although the temperature was mild, the overcast skies were not promising. I wrote until 7:00 a.m. and went back to bed for a nap. We both got up at 9:00 a.m. as the rain was producing sound effects as it fell upon our metal roof. Since there was no point in sitting and listening to the rain, we decided to continue our journey north. We didn't want family to be concerned so we continued to hunt for internet hot spots to send them texts. At 11:00 a.m., I commenced my initial test of preparing for departure in cool precipitation. Even though we planned to stay two nights at the Eight Flags Campground, the Manager issued a one-night refund without hesitation. The rain was light, the new rain gear worked well, and the unhooking process was not cumbersome.

The total mileage from home to the Canadian Border was 2,866 miles, all of them traveled without any difficulty or major gridlocks. Route planning to avoid major cities including, Chicago, St. Louis and Denver had been effective. At this point, we have traversed over twenty percent of our planned total mileage. That being said, I made my first error in finding my chosen route until after we passed it in the first half-hour of leaving the campground. My re-routing likely caused us an additional fifty miles and an added hour of travel.

After crossing the St. Mary River, we pulled into a lonely gas station to fuel up in Vauxhall, Alberta. When I asked the price per gallon (as the sign stated liters), the young female attendant very pleasantly suggested we travel to the next town for gasoline. She said: "I know you will be spending a lot in the big rig". We found her helpful counsel rather astonishing, and it was obvious she was just a kind individual. We will need to calculate the conversion rate, as we hadn't previously considered the need to do so.

Sunshine, beautiful cloud formations and a temperature of 57 degrees delighted us at 1:45 p.m. The landscape continued to be vast acres of cropland. We wondered what the 3-foot high and triangular peaked structures in the agricultural acres were. They were separated by approximately six feet, and were obviously intended to protect something but what they were protecting was a mystery.

It was pleasing to see two Pronghorns grazing peacefully in southern Alberta near the Bow River and Vow Slope Canal, which are, no doubt, utilized for irrigation. The landscape remained unchanged on Route #36 with thousands of acres of cropland, and small houses on farms separated by miles and with six to twelve silos at each. The investment in harvested crop storage far exceeded that of creature comfort.

We encountered absolutely spectacular cloud formations, which appeared to be much closer to the ground than we are accustomed to seeing. The clouds gave us the feeling of being totally surrounded and revealed the "Big Sky Country" concept. It was a serene sensation.

A road sign announced: "Silver Sage Community Corral" of to our east. Unfortunately, it was out of our view.

Very few vehicles accompanied us beyond Red Deer River. The traffic was so light that we pondered living in such isolation. We saw another sign for Finnegan Ferry and thought it was an odd name for this type of cropland. Occasionally, we read signs such as "Important Intersection Ahead" and "Rural Crime Watch". The absence of buildings and normal materialistic orientations evaporated and generated the feeling of releasing one's spirit to the Universe.

At 3:55 p.m., dramatic stormy skies appeared in the west, and we could see the precipitation erasing the sky. It was another awesome sight.

In "Two Hills", Alberta, we searched for our campground in the one-stoplight community. We were unsuccessful so we turned the motorhome around and entered a liquor retail establishment to ask for directions. The dirt road adjacent to the building was our answer - there had been no signs. In a quarter mile, we saw a travel trailer and a small golf course, which, as it developed, was the office for the campground. The young female clerk was very congenial and asked if we were planning to "stay and play". That type of terminology at a hotel in Nevada might have a much different interpretation! I reserved a tee time for 10:59 for the next morning. The campground had a total of seven sites with electric and water hook- ups. The practice putting green was directly behind our site #7. There was only one other camper on site #2. This was an absolutely perfect site to satisfy our preferences. It was void of neighboring RV's. a view of the golf course and adjacent trees. Even though it was 7:15 p.m., I lit the charcoal grill, built a campfire in our portable firepit, and set- up outdoor tables and chairs. Since it remains daylight until 9:30 p.m. and with the cool weather (low 50's) keeping the insects to a minimum, we enjoyed the outdoor environment for the evening. It was the perfect camping experience.

We drove 401 miles today.

DAY #12

The sunshine penetrating the window of the bed area awakened me at 5:30 a.m. I wrote until 7:00 a.m. while I relished my morning coffee. I went back to bed and set the clock for 8:30a.m.

My golf clubs are stored above the driver and passenger seats, an area originally designed for a children's sleeping area. With Nancy's help, I managed to prepare for our golf outing. The temperature continued to rise and the warmth prepared us for a glorious outing. On the first tee, I was delighted to find thick grass and a well-groomed fairway as I was expecting sparse conditioning. Nancy was smiling when I asked her to drive the cart. It was a pleasant learning curve for her to navigate the paths as my drives fortunately were mostly on the fairway, and easy to locate. The course wasn't crowded, and I was able to play the better of two balls. I scored two pars and one double bogey for a score of 44, which was a good round for me.

Before golfing and while eating our Cheerios, Nancy remarked: "Oh there are two small young animals playing in the grass in front of our motorhome. They have pointed noses and they are so cute. Maybe they are baby possums." When I saw them, I suggested they might be woodchucks. When we exited our "home away from home" we saw six or eight of them scrambling with lots of energy and popping up out of holes in the ground. We immediately decided that they were not either of our initial suspicions.

After golfing, we entered the Pro Shop and began conversing with Wendy. She was in her sixties and a very friendly Canadian. She related that she had a forty-year-old son who was very accomplished: An author, a musician, a competitive marksman and an online elementary school teacher (we had never heard of that occupation). She was obviously very proud of him. Her husband, also a native Canadian, is a farmer and mechanic. The couple and a nephew farm 1500 acres of wheat and lentils. When asked, she informed us that the "cute creatures" were gophers and that Alberta is inundated with them. "They multiply like rabbits and are a nuisance to farmers because each of them have their own hole in the ground. My husband shoots them with his 22". I suggested they might be cousins to ground hogs as they behave similarly as both of them stand on hind legs to look for intruders. We did not see them on the golf course: perhaps the weed killer spray was not conducive to their health.

The golf course was selling firewood for $15 per wheelbarrow load. When we made our purchase, she offered: "Take all you can load". We chose seventy pieces that would just fit in the exterior storage area with the existing camping gear. In comparison to eight pieces for $9 at Lowes or the gas station at home, we got a real bargain. Nancy also bought a "Two Hills" golf shirt for 35 Canadian dollars ($24 American). She said she didn't need it but wanted a souvenir memory of driving the golf cart, which we used to haul the wood to the motorhome.

We asked Wendy about the Amish family residing in campsite #2. She acknowledged they were Mennonites with six children and had been there for a month. She had known the family for many years while working at other locations and further related that she deemed their lifestyle as "sad". "They only educate their children through the fifth grade as they won't permit them to discover the outside world. They are taught to be afraid of individuals who are not Mennonites". We watched them entertaining themselves all afternoon with their one bicycle and sticks. They appeared to be very happy and extremely well mannered. However, they were very reluctant to socialize with us.

Wendy continued to educate us when we asked her about the 3-foot high structures we observed. They are covers for natural gas valves. Sulfur was the odor we smelled. On their farm, the wells generated yearly revenue of $3,600.

The wood we purchased produced a warm flame that evening as we dined on charcoal grilled salmon. We had a glorious adventure today and drove zero miles.

DAY #13

I wrote about our experiences from 5:30 a.m. to 7:30 a.in. Daylight at this location exists from 4:00 a.m. to 10:00 p.m., leaving only six hours of darkness. Interestingly, our bodies have adjusted to the external daylight as 5:00 a.m. feels like 7:00 a.m.

We planned to continue our journey the next day but had to wait until morning to pack up the outside gear, as the firepit must cool overnight. The fire pit has to be loaded first and then surrounded by the remaining table and chairs. Nancy stored the cooking and eating necessities inside.

The rubber hit the road at 9:00 a.m., and we welcomed excellent driving conditions. The route planned avoided Calgary and Edmonton, as we would rather look at the countryside than vehicles.

We had Route #36 north mostly to ourselves. Edging along the Saddle Lake Cree Nation, the topography changed to birch lined trees, which was vastly different than the croplands we traversed two days earlier. Lottie Lake and the Floating Stone Community came into view. At 9:50 a.m., we approached the beautiful Good Fish Lake, and I became concerned about the gas gauge being below one-quarter of a tank, as stations didn't operate on this lonely highway. We thought we could easily make it to Lac La Biche but we decided to take a three-mile side venture to Kikino, a two-pump facility. Expecting a price gouge, we only prepaid for $50, which provided a one-quarter tank of additional reserve. Feeling more relaxed; we arrived in Lac La Biche and found the gas to be only one penny per litre less expensive. The fill-up was $210. The small town had a country feel about it but there were no visible attractions.

We ventured westward once again on Route #55 and stopped for lunch in the motorhome at another beautiful lake in Athabasca. (At this point, we had only eaten at a restaurant once since leaving home). Children were running through a sprinkler in a city playground even though the temperature was only 72 degrees, while Nancy was wearing a sweatshirt to step outside and stretch her legs.

As we embarked on Route #2, we realized that we haven't seen a highway patrolman on these seldom traveled roads since we crossed the border. Prior to this day, we weren't aware that Alberta was bestowed with so many beautiful lakes and rivers, and we have enjoyed no fewer than 20 of them under and beside the roadways on this day alone.

We read signs alerting us to "Stock At Large" and "Logs May Swing Into Your Lane, Do Not Pass". Near "Grasslands", we were fortunate to see what might have been a young Moose with no antlers. The body was too thick and muscular to be a deer. The animal became confused when it reached the highway, back tracked, and then crossed the highway and gracefully jumped up a 4-foot bank into the trees. It was an experience we immensely enjoyed. We also spotted two mule deer during the day.

As our route changed from north to west, the cross wind changed to a tailwind enabling us to easily cruise at 70 miles per hour on this two-lane and sparsely trafficked road. We made good time and arrived at the Provincial Park Campground at 2:30 p.m. We did see the remnants of our second highway accident since we began our journey. A truck had jettisoned its load and unrolled bailing wire covered the high way shoulder. Highway Department employees were laboring to reload the wire. It looked like a difficult and potentially "cutting" effort. We felt blessed that we weren't following the truck when the load escaped and considered ourselves extremely fortunate since we have traveled over 3,000 miles.

Lesser Slave Lake campground is very remote, and each site is separated by natural vegetation. It reminded us of a campsite in Florida that we like.

We roasted hot dogs over our fire pit, and the newly purchased birch logs burned well. While enjoying the flames while sipping scotch and eating cashews; a brazen little squirrel was intent on pestering me for food for ten minutes. I chased him numerous times, and he or she persisted to return and was obviously not afraid of humans. It was a wonderful day with great weather, easy driving, excellent landscape, a nice campfire, and the joy of new experiences.

We drove 276 miles today.

DAY #14

L eaving Slave Lake, we spotted the first base-ball field we have seen in Canada. My activity on the diamond has been my lifelong passion. I played Little League at 12 and began playing Senior Softball at age 52. If interested, you can read about my adrenaline highs on Kindle Vella. My three National Championship watches will become the possession of my three grandchildren. The MVP and All-Star ribbons will no doubt perish with my demise, as it should be. I lived and treasured those moments but they have little meaning to anyone else. The early morning viewing also included a lonely deer grazing and Grizzly Bear Honda Car Dealership. It was an appropriate name for the latter as we were warned at our last campground to be on the alert for bears. While building a campfire, I holstered my C02 look-a-like Glock and unpackaged the bear spray. We are looking forward to that experience so long as it is from the inside of our motorhome.

Brilliant sunshine led the way beyond Caribou Trail, Mooney Creek, Sawridge First Nations, Canyon Creek, Assineau River, Big Lakes County, Eula Creek, Kinuso Area, Swan River, Strawberry Creek, Old Man Creek, Jim Cooks River, Driftpile Cree Nation, Driftpile River, Shadow Creek, Joussard Area, Sucker Creek First Nation, and Arcadia Creek. As the names imply, the landscape displayed nature's beauty for seemingly endless miles. However, it was obvious that it is not part of the Native American culture to take pride in the appearance of their properties. I n stark contrast, their very few visible homes are cluttered with "junk" and not one manicured lawn was seen in the Nations.

A sign pointed to a ski area to the east, and we wondered why an avid outdoor enthusiast would engage in that sport in this very flat topography? We seriously doubted that local residents frequented that area on Route #43.

At Woodpecker Creek, a sign read: "Watch For Pedestrians On The Highway". The highway had 4 lanes and 70 kilometer per mile speed limit. There were walkways under the highway similar to the golf course tunnels in the Villages in Florida to provide transit for walkers to "get to the other side". We had never seen that in our prior travels. In the "middle of nowhere", we did observe a middle-aged man wandering down the shoulder of the highway.

A gas station attendant, a pleasant woman in her forties, recommended that we visit Liard Springs. She noticed our North Carolina license plate and correctly assessed our Alaska destination. The topography dramatically changed as we descended into a steep ravine and then back up to a flat plateau. During the descent, and unexpected draft of wind shook and moved the vehicle quite vigorously. I gripped the steering wheel with both hands to control the movement of our heavy machine.

We arrived at the Dawson Creek Visitor Center at 2:30 p.m. (West Coast Time). The Mile Post Planning Book recommended this stop, and it was a valuable visit. Ipicked up eight or nine pieces of travel literature, which might make our trip more interesting. Dawson Creek is the beginning of the Alaska Highway, and the first city where we witnessed many tourists embarked on our same journey. I expected waiting lanes or traffic gridlock but there were neither. The four young women hosting the Visitor Center were a delight, and we shared a few laughs. A bumper sticker reading "Mile Post Zero" caught our eyes.

That day was the solstice, which meant that it was the longest day of the year, and we would not experience total darkness.

We conversed with a couple in their sixties at the RV Park who had traveled from Minnesota. They told us that they don't make park reservations and just travel until they feel the need to rest. Surprisingly, they hadn't had any difficulty securing a campground site. We wouldn't want to take that risk.

The large motorhome parked adjacent to us at Northern Lights RV Park accommodated a middle-aged couple who were leading a caravan of fourteen RVs through Alaska. Larry has led this tour for ten years and was a very knowledgeable source of Alaska information. RV'ers pay him to "show them the best way" to see the attractions. We didn't ask how much they pay but wished we had thought to ask. It would be impossible to overtake that group in the highway-passing lane!

We weren't permitted to have a campfire that night due to imposed fire restrictions. However, I did charcoal grill fish and sat outside until 10:00 p.m. in the daylight reading the literature I picked up at the Visitor Center.

Two weeks of being together 24/7 has revealed a new game score between us; Nancy 18 vs. Jim 15, 33 mental faux pas seemed exorbitant but we prevail most happily.

We drove 310 miles today.

DAY #15

W hile dumping and un-hooking the electric and water, I engaged the neighbor Larry and was informed that he charges $13,000 to each of the campers included in his caravan. The cost includes 4 boat trips and many meals.

Upon reflection, I realized those campers enjoy a valuable service in the event of mechanical or operational difficulties as well as socialization with like-minded individuals. I asked for his business card and plan to send him a copy of this narrative when it is published.

The walking tour map of Dawson Creek highlighted a coffee and baked goods shop named "Mugs and Hugs". Our taste buds were craving a good breakfast treat: cinnamon muffins, are our favorite. We were disappointed to find that it did not open until 9:00 a.m. The owner misses a lot of revenue by not accommodating early morning travelers. Given the 18-20 hours of daylight, we saw a number of travelers leaving the campground before 6:00 a.m. A little advertising could capture their income before they start up the Alaska Highway.

When the Alaska Highway was constructed during WWII, the master by- way was an engineering marvel. It was a joint effort by the United States and Canadian governments whose purpose was to support military defenses on the West Coast in the event of a Japanese attack. Congress approved the expenses for the project only five days after it was proposed with the United States paying the total cost for the highway, and Canada becoming a beneficiary. Our current Congress would squabble for months before passing such a positive decision for Americans. More than 11,000 soldiers and engineers, 16,000 civilians and 7,000 pieces of construction equipment completed the 1500 mile road in less than nine months: Today it takes two years to construct new lanes of Interstate #26 near Asheville.

Shortly after crossing the Kiskatinaw River, we began a steep descent of 10 degrees into a lush valley and ravine. While gearing down to reduce brake shoe wear, we were excited to see a Moose at the edge of the Birch trees on the other side of the south bound lanes. He or she appeared to be contemplating the risk of crossing. Some of them do not make it across successfully as we saw three dead ones on the highway during our travels that day.

The plume from an oil refinery blazed the horizon near Charlie's Lake.

Approximately 80 miles north, we viewed the results of a large-scale fire that contaminated the air quality all the way into the United States. The burned vegetation continued for 20 miles. At Halfway River First Nation, a dangerous driver (#7) passed our vehicle and another RV on a blind uphill solid yellow line. At Mile Marker 109, we encountered a completely desolate area. There were no vehicles within sight for a distance of four miles ahead, no building sites of any variety, and nature was at its peak. Our spirits were constantly uplifting with beautiful terrain around every bend and up and down every slope. On three different occasions that day, vehicular traffic was stopped by a flagman, as the road was limited to one-lane traffic to accommodate road repair. It appeared that water run-off from the mountain had created concrete erosion, and a plastic pipe with a large diameter was being buried on the shoulder of the road to divert the damaging element of nature off the surface of the road. Another construction circumstance near the top of Pink Mountain created the nearest pedestrian collision that we have ever experienced. Our motorhome was the only stopped vehicle in either direction, and when we were given the signal to proceed slowly, the uphill climb limited our speed to a school zone limit. We were proceeding in the left lane with orange cones on our right side when a construction worker bolted from the left shoulder directly in to our pathway. He was waving frantically to the driver of a construction grader to arrest his motion to no avail. The darting worker was wearing a white hard hat and yellow vest and appeared to be an Engineering Supervisor in his forties. I had the brake pedal depressed and the horn blaring. The worker did not even look in our direction and didn't heed the alert. He was totally focused and intent on preventing any further deleterious movement by the driver of the construction grader. Our front bumper actually grazed his overalls and, despite the near tragedy, he was impervious to his well-being. We don't think he ever realized that our vehicle existed despite our squealing brakes and blaring horn. Nancy and I were in momentary shock and halted for a few seconds to allow our hearts to start beating once more. I was motivated to exit my driver's seat and say a few words but, by now, a fifth-wheel was waiting behind us. A turn-off to park our vehicle was not available, and we didn't want to impede that vehicle's progress. Both of our mental faculties were overcome with the incident for a few miles. Interestingly, we both had the same visualization: A man falling to the concrete and out of sight under our front bumper. The mental scene was surreal and remained with me as I wrote about the near tragedy eighteen hours later. Had I not been able to stop our vehicle in time, our adventure would have changed dramatically. Laws protect construction workers and, no doubt, the investigating law enforcement agency would have arrested me for negligent driving. Void any witnesses, my defense would have been insufficient, as Nancy's testimony would have been deemed biased. The remainder of the driving for that day was devoted to caution rather than exhilaration. Nancy did compliment me on my quick perhaps lifesaving, reaction. I am blessed at age 86 to have physical prowess. When I was sixteen, my hometown newspaper (The Ledger) referred to me with a headline: "Quick Witted Youth Saves Life". This is mentioned in another Kindle Vella story I wrote under the pen name of "Sportyman".

The terrain of Moose Flats included a sign, which welcomed Moose hunters, but crossing Bucking Horse River did not generate the spiritual excitement we anticipated. The adrenaline-producing event we experienced yesterday remained all encompassing. Very large cranes came in to view as we crossed Bucking Horse River. A new bridge was under construction and gave me pause about the one-lane traffic crossing. Would it be safe?

We registered at "Triple G Hideaway RV Park at 2:00 p.m. and retired for an afternoon nap to retool our mentality. We had no previously assigned site but there were many sites open but choosing one was not an option for us. The registration ladies were not personable, and the site we were assigned was gravel with no grass and charcoal grilling was not permitted. In regard to the latter, we believed they were trying to entice patrons to use their dining room. It was not a satisfactory camping experience.

We drove 290 miles today.

DAY #16

We departed at 9:00 a.m. under overcast dark skies, and the only restaurant that was open had no baked goods. We were then greeted by miles of burned forest with fresh ashes covering the earth and, no doubt, the cause of the smoky air in the campground where we stayed the previous night.

We came upon stopped traffic- and our excitement abounded when we discovered it was due to a young mother black bear and her cub grazing the mountainside shoulder of the highway and completely undisturbed by approaching vehicles. Hopefully, Nancy's photos will do them justice. As the elevation increased and the temperature dropped to 49 degrees, the increasing fog became precarious. Visibility was less than a car length, and the only guide was the dull yellow line in the middle of the black top. Even driving at a 15 mile per hour speed, we felt unsafe. We both breathed a sigh of relief when we descended enough to take control of our navigation again. The trepidation vanished as we arrived at the beautiful Summit Lake at the base of Stone Mountain.

We stopped at Toad River Lodge to fill the gas tank and got ripped off, as expected, as the cost to fill up was the most we had paid to date: $263.88. We purchased sweet rolls and found them to be tasty even at $6.00 Canadian. I examined the breakfast menu and chuckled when I saw a 2 eggs and toast breakfast for $19.95!

The highway was very "wavy", and we were jostled up and down and all around as the unintended slopes in the pavement dictated. Muncho Lake might be the most inspiring body of water we have ever marveled, and a sign for McDonald Campground was inviting. After driving 4 hours in light to medium rainfall, the skies began to clear at 1:00 p.m. We were tired of the slick high ways and mountain terrain. The rapidly flowing white water created rapids in the Liard River. We had planned to visit the Hot Springs but the rain deterred us. WE will try again on the return route from Alaska. The white water reminded us of the movie "River Wild" which starred Meryl Streep and Kevin Bacon. It was necessary to remain alert, as recent rockslides had deposited good-sized rocks on the highway, one of which was quite massive. We enjoyed seeing three different herds of Bison ranging in size up to twenty each. Six or eight young calves were included, and some of them were nursing. The monster Bull was demonstrating his control as he removed the smaller ones from his path with his head and horns.

As we entered the Province of Yukon, the odometer turned and revealed that we had traveled 4,762 miles since leaving home.

Prior to entering the campground, we visited the Northern Lights Theatre and watched two 20-minute movies in a Planetarium setting. One was created by a Denver Research Organization and explained the importance of "Black Holes" in our cosmos in a vivid pictorial fashion. It was very interesting. The other depicted the nature of the Northern Lights phenomenon. Unfortunately, June was not the appropriate time to view and experience the spectacle.

Registering at the campground on Watson Lake was an absolute disaster! The man standing ahead of me was discussing a receipt problem with the clerk who was an overweight man in his sixties. He had been given the incorrect receipt and site assignment to a previously registered camper who was already hooked -up. When that confusion terminated, it was my turn to become frustrated. The clerk insisted that I didn't have a reservation and produced a hand scribbled list of names, which did not include mine. I went back to the motorhome to gather my records as he suggested that I had reserved another campground. Although I had not received an email confirmation as is typical with campground reservations, he accepted my submittal. He was unapologetic and rude but did assign me a site. The campground had RV's cramped in like anchovies in a can and was all gravel without a blade of grass in sight. There wasn't any view or motivation to sit outdoors.

We drove 325 miles today, and our game score is Nancy 21 and Jim only 16.

DAY #17

I t is our first day in the Providence of Yukon, Canada and our first stop is Watson Lake. It is the home of the Laird First Nation and "Signpost Forest". The forest was originated by an army soldier busy building the Alaska Highway in 1942. He posted a sign to point the way home to Danville, Illinois. Tourists since then have added their signs to total over 100,000 nameplates. It is a remarkable spectacle and would take days to examine in total. We slowly eased by to marvel at the sight.

We were curious when eyeing an advertisement for a movie on the Northern Lights. Since we cannot view in June, we seated ourselves with only two others to receive the education. It was well done and interesting.

The Alaskan Highway, Rt. #1, mileage was originally 1,422 miles and completed in less than nine months. The U.S. Government authorized the construction in 3 days after receiving the request. Today it requires two plus years to complete new lanes on 126 near Asheville, North Carolina. The army utilized 11,0 00 men, 5,000 trucks, 904 tractors, and 374 graders working 12-16 hours per day to accomplish the task. The highway was a deterrent to the enemy in World War II to attack the region. It was then given to Canada.

The population of the Yukon is 43,568, and home to 218,000 porcupine caribou, named for the

Porcupine River, which bisects the herd range from East to West. The moose herd is estimated at 70,000.

With overcast skies and drizzling rain, it was two hours before we approached the first vehicle. A strong sense of isolation is a strange feeling. Twenty-five miles south of Teslin we see snow to the west on the mountain peaks.

Our first tourist attraction in Teslin was the Tlingit Heritage Center. Just prior to entering the village we spied huge cranes in the sky, which was startling given this remote pristine wilderness. The scenic landscape sits on Nisutlin Bay and Teslin Lake. Teslin in the Tlingit culture means "Long Narrow Water". A new bridge is under construction replacing the longest bridge on the Alaska Highway reaching 1,916 feet: Longer than six football fields. With a flagman and one-lane crossing I was silently pondering the worthiness of the structure. The construction is scheduled to be completed in 2026 at an estimated cost of $1,200,000. The lake is 78 miles long, 2 miles wide, and 700 feet in depth. The salmon travel north thru the lake to go home and spawn. Population of Teslin is 486: The bridge receives very little local traffic.

At the Heritage Center we parked in front of four interesting 10-foot-high totem poles: A can't miss photo opportunity. A sign on the door reads, "Opens at 9:00 a.m.", however another sign is labeled "Closed" I turned the knob and the door opened. We were greeted by a young Native American woman who informed us that a young woman was recently killed in a traffic accident and their small community was ceasing most activities in remembrance. She invited us to walk thru the exhibits without paying, as the displays would not be operable. While doing so we greeted two elderly Tlingit Natives eating lunch. Our friendly smiles disarmed their stern body language, and quickly they disclosed their cultural reverence for the deceased.

Following a brief interchange we ventured onto the George Johnson Museum. A young woman, perhaps in her early twenties and a young boy both rose from their seats on the porch to welcome us. That was a pleasant surprise at a museum. They were both extremely reserve although welcoming. Recording our payment of $6 each, she asked if we would like an "Introductory Explanation" of the museum: That was our second pleasant surprise. Of course, we responded yes, and she related a brief story of George's life and his considerable contribution to the development of Teslin.

We found her, and her brother's humble and warm personalities refreshing, and a distinct contrast to the societal environment we call home. She only attended public school through fifth grade and graduated high school online.

Her nature continued to be meek and unassuming, while the young man didn't utter a word. We received their presence as humble and warm: A refreshing contrast to the majority of teenagers I meet during societal outings.

The museum was a treasure of local culture accompanied by an explanation of each display and picture. What a mistake it would have been to bypass this attraction, as I often do with museums. George Johnson Museum is the home of the first vehicle (1928 Chevy) arriving in Teslin. George had it floated down the river from Whitehorse, before there was a road built in this community. It has been restored and is in brand new appearing condition.

Further inquiry revealed the girl's age of nineteen. She was born in Pennsylvania very near Nancy's home of Selinsgrove. Her father was reared Mennonite and now is a non-denominational church leader. That explains her and her brother's reserve nature (parenting). She only attended public school through the fifth grade and graduated high school "online". She plans to enter a Christian College in the fall with the goal of becoming a Christian Counselor following in her father's footsteps.

Our Teslin visit was a super introduction to a distant neighbor: most enjoyable 3.5 hours.

While fueling "Perser" I observed an elderly native Tlingit woman selling marijuana to a young man.

Driving beside the solid rock border on the shoulder of the road once again is energizing, as we progress to Whitehorse.

We registered at Pioneer RV Park at 2:00 p.m. and were delighted with our campsite in the trees. After napping I built a campfire for the evening and charcoal grilled salmon. The campsites on top of the hill were spacious and adequately separated to provide a pleasant "living environment". Site #130 was a jewel, even without sewer: Can always use the dump station when needed. The campsites below the hill with sewer had no trees and were very close to their neighbor.

We drove 277miles and experienced a great day of travel.

DAY #12

The population of Whitehorse is 34,881: Three quarters of the providence population, and is the capitol.

Assembled an early morning campfire with branches cut from the trees already dead on the ground. Loaded additional kindling in the storage area for future pleasure. While Nancy enjoyed her "sleepin", I am authoring beside the flames: Very pioneering sensation. Authentic camping experience as the flames cooked our scrambled eggs, with cheese, and bacon.

First stop on the day was Miles Canyon on the Yukon River. Centuries ago the erupted lava formed volcanic rock which created sponge textured basalt. When cooling quickly the molten rock generates columns uniquely visible in the canyon.

Proceeded to the wildlife refuge park. Walking tour was procurable, however upon inspection we determined it would be too arduous for our "mature" frames: We made a good decision a one-hour bus ride with a narration by the driver was considerably more comfortable. Cost was only eight dollars each, and we were the only patrons on the vehicle: A personalized tour. We covered 70 acres of penned caribou, moose, Dall sheep and our favorite tinhorn sheep, mountain goats, and musk ox.

We then ventured to the Nordic Hot Springs 17 miles from town: The only hot springs in the Yukon. It is a very modern facility with zero historic ambiences. Featuring three Japanese style rock pools, a cold plunge pool, two saunas and two steam rooms, heated cement loungers, Hamam-style beds, and fire pit seating. Cost is $48 each.

The showers were very disappointing, as they were designed to preserve water. After turning the knob, water only emerged for 10 seconds. Darting in and out was not relaxing, rather distasteful as the water temperature was impossible to regulate.

The parking lot would not accommodate RV's and I found a dead end with little space to turn around. Signage was not visible to prevent the discomfort.

Eventually located a gravel entranceway with a long walk to the facility.

DAY #19

Another day of tourism in Whitehorse, which the Guinness World Records states is the least air polluted city in the world. Awakening at 6:00 a.m. afforded me the opportunity to saw more kindling in the adjacent woods, before Nancy was up and about. Our agenda includes six attractions in the center city area, with a pleasant temperature of 59 degrees.

We were disappointed that the S.S. Klondike Sternwheeler was closed for repairs: We could only view the exterior. The "Dam and Fish Ladder" as a result were our highlight. The Ladder provides an avenue for the salmon to avoid the dam, and a tank like environment provides a clear inspection for visitors. Chinook salmon spawn in the Yukon River, and during their first year of life live in freshwater, migrating eventually downstream to the Bearing Sea off the coast of Alaska, then Navigate for two to six years in salt water before returning to their birthplace. The swim of 1,864 miles is the longest migration run in the world. In recent years the harvest of this tasty meal has continued to decrease.

The Whitehorse Wharf on the Yukon River is home to the Mac Bride Museum. Photographs of the Gold Rush era, and a wild life display enrich this visit.

Kwanlin Dun Cultural Center is nearby. The heritage of the native first nation people is well documented. An old Log Anglican Church standing down town bestows a photograph occasion. Watching the world's largest weathervane and original Canadian Pacific Airlines DC-3 passenger plane turn as the wind dictates is a unique experience.

Subsequent to our very interesting downtown exploration we took advantage of the laundry at Pioneer RV Park. This campground offers most every feature a traveler fancies: Even a specific location for a vehicle oil change. After filling the propane tank, we agonized with our first motorhome non-performance, as the refrigerator would not remain in operation. The "check" light persisted in beeping; Nancy read the owner's manual as is her natural inclination without success. (I rarely read manuals based on previous lack of prospering). Frustrated and relenting to the possibility of requiring an RV Repair Center. I fortunately benefitted as my brain enlightened me to a possible remedy. I plugged the electric cord to the external source and was relieved to witness the silence. Not understanding why I was successful, necessitates asking the question to more experienced RV'ers.

Unfortunately the ensuing rain pre-empted my campfire plans and I defaulted to naptime. When the rain ceased at 9:30 p.m., I continued to saw wet firewood and pack in the RV storage compartment. I am amazed at the amount of travel "stuff" I can load; Very adequate. It is a new experience to utilize daylight at 10:30 p.m.

Game score: Nancy 19 - Jim 17

DAY # 20

Destination is Beaver Creek, Yukon. The campgrounds are first come first serve, therefore we departed on our 284-mile day at 5:30 a.m. The early morning yielded a moose sighting grazing on the edge of the woods. We grasped the "Milepost" recommended breakfast at the Village Bakery in Haines Junction. Once again the signage was weak and we had to hunt to find it on a side street. The pothole gravel parking lot was severely tilted and the motorhome was uneasy as we parked. (She has been dubbed "Perser", short for Perseverance as the rough and uneven surfaces she endures deserves credit). The cinnamon breakfast rolls were very good and "Perser" was a comfortable setting for nourishment. Fortunately the entrepreneur recognized the business opportunity and opened at 7:00 a.m. We arrived at 7:15 a.m. and there were 8 or 10 other consumers arriving as well in the small building, where only six seats were provided. Thanks to the "Milepost" book otherwise it would have been a missed local treat.

We encountered a 10-minute flagman delay due to road construction, which is severely needed.

Our sighting of a grizzly mother and two cubs "made our day", as Clint Eastwood made famous. They were grazing in knee-high grass just off the left shoulder of the highway: Two other vehicles were stopped and the occupants taking pictures. We had a clear view as no vehicles were coming towards us in the other lane. All three wild life were undisturbed by our presence. That changed immediately when two motorcycles approached from our rear. The loud noise, unfamiliar to the bears, immediately cautioned one cub to rise on its hind legs to investigate the intruder. Quickly thereafter the mother did the same. Nancy got a good picture of the cub standing. It was an exciting moment for us to behold, although fleeting, and a forever memory in our lives.

Immediately all three scurried into the woods. In bear safety films we had been informed that loud noise can motivate bears to retreat, and we just witnessed that evidence.

I have determined that the holes in the highway as labeled "pot" are not appropriate names. They are more like two-man foxholes, which could include two browning automatic rifles. The, never know when, dips and waves in the road surface has reduced our speed to 35 MPH. Keeping "Perser" afloat is now a priority: earnestly it is a challenge not welcomed.

We witnessed our eighth dangerous driver, as a motorhome passed us and a second vehicle on the brink of a hill on a solid yellow line. Had an oncoming vehicle been climbing that slope, an accident could not have been avoided. I pressed the brake pedal to assure we wouldn't become a recipient of someone else's poor decision.

The "first come first serve" identification by Milepost was no longer valid, as one campground was tent only and the second was boondocking only and the third was closed as the owner had suffered a heart attack. Therefore we continued up "Bobber Road", as I labeled it, to the U.S. Customs Border in Alaska. At 2:15 p.m. we found a single female investigative officer and we were eighth in line. The wait was only twelve minutes as the interviews were all short. She inspected our passports and asked about firearms and firewood. Her initial body language was somber and strict, however changed to a smile after her initial greeting. I am not sure, however perhaps my U.S.M.C. hat helped? Odometer mileage indicated 5,150 miles traveled to arrive in our 49th state as of January 3, 1959.

We entered Sourdough Campground in Tok, Alaska at 4:00 p.m. and were invited to the pancake toss at the pavilion at 7:30 p.m. A nap and soup preceded our attendance. The owner, a man in his forties conducted his innovated attraction, and while his sense of humor was interactive with twenty-two guests was refreshing, the "toss" was less amusing. A rubberish material shaped like a pancake was directed to be thrown into a bucket. If successful, a token ten percent discount on breakfast was the reward. One young man mastered the challenge.

Disappointingly, the current Alaska wildfire has created a ban on campfires.

Today's drive of 422 miles felt like a pilgrimage, and wasn't our most pleasant. However, the bears sighting provides a treasurable memory to "sleep on".

DAY # 21

With a name such as "Sourdough", having a pancake breakfast with reindeer sausage was an attractive option in the campground restaurant. We took advantage of the High Water Pressure Wash, it was four dollars (two wash cycles) and "Perser" looked more presentable.

The Alaska Dept. of Transportation advises motorists of the highway condition with "rough patch" signage. The Yukon Govt. apparently isn't as considerate, although their retail prices merit a traveler's recognition: Easily 20 to 30 percent higher than prices in the U.S.

Our first Alaskan picturesque scene is Shaw Lake, although the "Bobber" highway doesn't afford the driver the opportunity to take his eyes from the concrete surface. Bobbing without the apples, limits the fun.

More flagman with ten-minute delays, then a pilot car leads the way on the open lane. Another dangerous driver, number nine passed on double yellow line with zero visibility. As we approach Eielson Air Force Base, we appreciate our initial four lanes on the Alaska Highway. We then cross Mrs. Claus Bridge.

I am quite disappointed approaching that major city of Fairbanks, as it appears no different than any other industrial city in the U.S. I was expecting scenery, however it doesn't exist: Neither igloos or bears in view. The Rivers Edge Campground was also a disappointment, with zero appeal and only gravel footing in the sardine packed campsites. The campground name is most certainly misleading. The cost of $56.10 is an outright gouging! Therefore, I plan to search for a more appealing location tomorrow.

From home to Fairbanks was 5,474 miles, and is our northernmost destination. Our journey was 215 miles today on the Alcan Highway, now "self-labeled" as Bobber Highway or "slow as you go" highway.

The Land of the Midnight Sun" offered many interesting attractions amid the colorful murals painted on many building exteriors, and even some steam pipes. The sculptures, which appeared on the sidewalks, added a pleasant feeling. Boasting continuous daylight for seventy consecutive days affords the opportunity to tee off on the golf course at 10:00 p.m.

DAY #22

Our first stop in Fairbanks was the Morris Thompson Cultural and Visitors Center, and it was rewarding. We secured loads of literature on attractions and watched a Bear Safety movie. The antler-constructed arch sets a tone for probing the expanse. The natives utilize caribou antlers, moose hide, whale baleen (filter feeding system). and walrus to sustain their lifestyle. The very detailed city map provided the knowledge to plot our route of exploration. A three-hour "River Boat Discovery" cruise on the Chena River at a cost of $90 each was our number one priority. The paddle vessel probably seated 300 to 400 passengers (excellent profit business). Salmon Dip, made with smoked salmon and cream cheese on a cracker, was served and after tasting we purchased some. The ride on the river was pleasant, although not exceptional. However, after docking at an island, the native cultural village demonstrations were very informative and interesting. The guides we met were all native to the local region and easily conversive. Their contributions generated a more than satisfactory value for the personal expense, as we walked, watched, questioned, and listened for over an hour.

A seaplane pilot displayed his skills for our benefit as he landed and rose again from the slow moving river. Seaplanes are numerous in Alaska as a primary mode of travel. Lake Hood, just south of town is the largest seaplane base in the U.S. From the boat we watched Alaskan sled dogs pull their load on a circular route. Probably 40 dogs were boarded there and puppies are trained for their life's work The temperature was in the high sixties and the dogs were hot after their demonstration. I was surprised to observe how excited and anxious they were to make their run. The guide disclosed that they naturally work at their peak at below 0 temperatures. Alaskan huskies are a cousin to the huskie pets in the southern states. Following their run, they darted to the river to cool off, at top speed. It was a most pleasurable experience to watch them work as they were trained from birth. The trainers and sled drivers were young girls, who verbalized the operation with clarity and expertise. The dogs also returned a good value on the $90 each expense.

Third visit was the large animal research station, operated by the University of Alaska, and included a guided tour at $18 each. The young woman, not native, was also well versed in the animal's natural behaviors. Our favorite was the musk ox, which I have never previously seen. We also saw reindeer with velvet-covered antlers. These animals look considerably different than the deer I watch crossing number 8 fairway from my home patio.

DAY #23

O ur first visit today is Pioneer Park, and once again I was pleasantly surprised. The admission is free and the 44-acre village celebrates the past with "Gold Rush" type buildings exhibiting the native local culture. Included is the Wickersham House built in 1904 and relocated to add to the Park's charm. Unfortunately the antique Stanley Steamer was closed for repairs. Observing only from the exterior, it exhibited my appeal to inspect the interior, as even the large size gave me an intense feeling to be a passenger.

Our exploration led us to "happen upon" an extremely "one of a kind" movie presentation in the round. An artist's drawings depicted the Gold Rush days which was appealingly narrated and labeled as the "stampede", only cost $4. Being as only six visitors were in attendance, we were able to leisurely converse with the operations manager. (Seating capacity was probably 100 and we prospered with no crowds or waiting in line to enter), He has lived in Fairbanks *over* fifty years and related stories of his young life in this "very different" culture; telling us that -50°F is not unusual to wake up to in the winter months. (Why would anyone choose to live there)?

The park advertised a "Salmon Bake" dinner at $35 per person. The sockeye fish was a big disappointment. I much prefer the Chinook taste we buy at our local grocery store.

We took the time today to get an oil change for "Perser" as she deserved that treat.

Final stop was at the American Legion Post. My Marine Corp's enlistment provides my qualification to membership. It is always enlightening to visit those retreats when traveling. Have many conversations with strangers who bond, based on their military backgrounds. It was novel to discover this post lacked a serving of scotch. Somewhat chagrined they offered me bourbon at no cost.

Neglected to mention that we partook of the "Milepost" suggestion to include the "Cookie Jar" restaurant in our travels. It wasn't a good experience as the waiting line was 25 minutes and the serving time was 45 minutes. Two tour busloads arrived prior and created our discomfort. Additionally it is very difficult to locate, as signage doesn't exist.

Twenty minutes south of Fairbanks is the town of North Pole, where the streetlight poles are decorated as candy canes. Not only is it known for its name, it also is home to the largest Christmas retail store (Santa Claus House) I have ever shopped. I couldn't resist purchasing a few items for my 15-month-old great grandson who lives in Chicago. We also chose two Alaskan tree ornaments.

DAY #24

We ventured north about 10 miles to capture a glimpse of the 800-mile Alaska Pipeline. Next was the Fountain Head Antique Auto Museum where we were stunned by an array of perhaps sixty vehicles dating to the early twenties thru the late thirties, and most of them had been restored to their original appeal: Very handsome display.

We resettled at the KOA at $70 per night and found this site to be rated poor. It is the northernmost KOA in the U.S.

DAY # 25

My phone had alerted me to the Riley Fire at Denali National Park. We approached with optimism though, as a traveler and the KOA office both told us the Park was open. To our dismay, as we approached, we could see the billowing black smoke covering the blue sky. The entrance road was barricaded and a Park Ranger was announcing to all would be visitors that no date had been signaled as the re-opening. It was at this juncture the biggest disappointment of the bucket list adventure. Viewing the wildlife I had read about for years was the pinnacle highlight I was anticipating.

Spotting a lone moose in a bog was quite exciting before arriving in Denali: Nearly adjacent in another bog a mother moose and her calf were lounging. (A Bog is a body of water that is covered by Sphagnum Moss, and sometimes labeled as a quagmire). We were able to pull to the shoulder and Nancy procured great pictures, which she sent to family members.

Our reserved campground for two nights was only a few miles further and judged appealing as we entered Grizzly Bear Campground. However reaching our campsite our emotions were drastically altered. With very little space to maneuver the back-in was difficult and perilous due to the heavily slanted surface. After four turns and accompanied reverses we settled between sparse trees. The highway was close to our rear bumper, and campers were walking between our "Perser" and the highway. They were aiming for the campground store, and therefore we were "able" to watch them return as well. We immediately knew this visit would be reduced to one highly undesirable night. I requested a refund, however was informed that policy did not exist.

This experience coupled with many others generates my consideration of traveling without reservations. During this journey, to my surprise, we found very few full campgrounds and many boon dockers (camping void of electric and water hook-ups). In Canada and Alaska, distinct from the lower 48 states, boondocking locations were plentiful as many recreation areas provided first come first serve RV sites; of course your unit needs to be equipped with a generator, water storage tank, and take your sleeping bag for nightly comfort without a heater. Paying for a campsite which is miserable is not rewarding. Despite the "crowd" at the campsite, I charcoal grilled, however we ate inside.

DAY #26

We are continuing south today without a reservation, given we departed the Denali area a day early. Hoping to find a pleasant campground before others arrive (also leaving Denali due to the fire) we pulled-out at 5:30 a.m. After inspecting and rejecting two campgrounds, Nancy noticed a sign identifying "Nancy Lake State Recreation Area", with a picture of a travel trailer which means camping, however no indication of mileage to arrive.

Speculating the name was a good omen we drove and drove and became less optimistic with every five minutes. Finally, after 5 miles we spotted a sign stating "South Rally Campground." It was first come first serve and we drove for fifteen minutes searching for an available site. We discovered only one and it was superb: Isolated from other campers, level, loads of vegetation and boulder at our rear bumper (strength!) Driving back to the entrance to pay our "good honor fee" ($20) in a machine, we were concerned that another camper would avail themselves of "our find". However, upon returning we backed in and set up our tables and chairs with a sigh of satisfaction. Not having electric or water did not decrease our comfort, and we brought to light that boondocking was a satisfactory camping experience, and in this instance much superior to an expensive KOA. Our three-hour campfire and lookout was relaxing. The campground embodied a very stunning wilderness lake and we noticed swimmers with tubes walking to enjoy at 58 degrees. Our good fortune in finding this inexpensive and appealing campsite significantly reduced our disappointment at Denali. We were in Willow, about 50 miles north of Anchorage.

The drive on Route #3 today was very scenic with the river bordering both sides of the road and snow appearing on the mountains beyond. Having departed in the early morning we had hoped and expected to view wild life, however that did not occur.

Nancy voiced her perturbance with the camper who placed their pink chair on the campsite across the road from us, and then did not arrive to utilize the site. We observed other campers on this July fourth eve holiday driving in search of an available site in this full recreation area, only to feel disappointment.

DAY #27

Highlighting our drive to Anchorage I delighted in one of my top three lifetime views, as we approached the city of Wasilla the earth stunningly and abruptly revealed a "dead ahead" solid rock formation. I was breathless for a couple of seconds as the Chugach and Talkeetna Mountain ranges divulged, amidst the clouds and scanty water vapor, a sight that rivaled a "vision" (planning the future with wisdom). The amplified sensation of "mountain highs" experiences includes Telluride, Colorado and Jackson Hole, Wyoming. Being July 4th, my son's birthday, imparted an additional significance.

The holiday parade in downtown prompted street closures and minor grid lock prior to locating our campground. Having reserved two nights to provide the opportunity to explore the attractions of Alaska's "big city", we were devastated when identifying our campsite in Centennial Park (box of chocolates). A multi-tented reunion was occurring directly across the street. Perhaps thirty families and seventy-five humans were totally oblivious to the peaceful environment anticipated by the other one hundred campers. Hoping to relocate, we visited the office and were disappointed to read a typewritten sign "management on the grounds will return soon" (that sign remained for the duration of our residence). The phone was unanswerable as well. Other campers disclosed they were also unimpressed with the absentee management. All evening the reunion children continuously traveled our campsite to reach the playground.

Watching the fireworks was on our agenda, however when we learned the event would take place at midnight, we abandoned that plan as our bodies tire before that hour: Very disconcerting experience.

DAY # 28

Feeling 57° this morning it was just a bit too chilly to sit outside with my coffee and pen, thus I am writing inside with the absence of noise as the children are still sleeping: Enjoying the peacefulness, eleven attractions have garnered my attention as I plan our tourist agenda. The city map is cumbersome for route planning.

Our initial priority today is watching the salmon journey upstream to spawn. That objective, surprisingly, engrossed us for one and a half hours inspecting the flowing water of Ship Creek: Finally allayed when we discovered eight to twelve clustered near the walkway at the fish hatchery. That establishment was very informative with scores of posters illuminating the operation, which embodies numerous plastic tanks containing thousands of salmon and trout. The tanks are located a floor below the viewing area with open tops: A very different approach for the excursionist.

During the salmon "hunt" we greeted a couple that reside in Virginia and they apprised us of an attraction at the Federal building downtown, which includes exhibits and an interesting movie. Unfortunately when we attempted to enter, the door was locked: Reason undisclosed.

The gathered tourist literature schooled us that "Rusty", an experienced Iditarod competitor, could be available on Main Street to engage in conversation. He was extremely personable and his many stories captured our absorption.

The Iditarod Trail was labeled as such; given it was the largest city between Nome and Nenana at the time of the diphtheria outbreak in 1925. Dog sleds traversed this ground to deliver serum. Twenty teams of dogs relayed the 600 miles.

When driving by the airpark we observed perhaps a thousand small airplanes, as private aircraft is preferred for transportation to the vehicle mode.

At $18 per person I opted not to tour the university's museum, as I expected the exhibits were primarily native culture and felt I was already well versed. Multiple tour buses were awaiting the return of their passengers and conversation with a couple of them indicated their pleasure with the experience. We then drove through the university's campus and Nancy photographed our visit.

DAY # 29

Woke to drizzling rain and fifty-five degrees, thus we decided to continue south to Moose Creek. The one-hundred mile drive provides numerous points of interest, as the Milepost book informs. As we departed the campground we tried the office once again to proclaim our displeasure; to no avail. We did read a hand written notice advising "bear seen in campground last night".

Our first visit was the O'Malley Golf Course. I was somewhat surprised to enter an upscale clubhouse and inspect a well-conditioned putting green, although slightly parched. The posted fees were consistent with Alaska's elevated cost of living; Eighty dollar green fees plus twenty-four dollars for a private cart. A likely comparable course in Waynesville or Haysville, N.C. would be approximately fifty percent of that total. Pull carts were available to scale the many visible steep fairway slopes. The last tee time of the day was listed as 9:56 p.m. Those golfers would be exiting the course at 2 a.m. That lifestyle is most difficult to conceive, despite the availability of increased daily yield.

Next on our agenda is Potter Marsh. As we parked "Perser" in a semi-crowded lot, we were alerted to a ferocious wind bending the small trees. Most tourists were bundled in winter coats and hooded garments. A couple of men were walking in short sleeves. The contrast provided us a chuckle. Nancy chose to cover her head and zip her coat before entering the boardwalk. Neither of our binoculars could locate any form of wildlife, as apparently it was too windy even for waterfowl.

We have been quite fortunate as this 51° wet day has been the first day we have endured inclement weather. The recall elevates our appreciation for the first four weeks of this journey. The rain is welcome to combat the dry conditions and threatening wildfires.

Experiencing dramatic transformations encompassing snow covered mountain peaks, serene lakes, rapidly flowing rivers, deep gorges and ravines, grassland valleys, as well as tall grass plains, has generated exhilaration for both Nancy and myself. Anticipating more of the same in the days ahead.

The traffic today is probably the heaviest we have encountered in Alaska, however void of gridlock. The weather no doubt contributes to the increase, as speed is reduced. For a stretch of thirty to forty miles we have been bordering a very long body of water on our right and beyond a towering mountain. The water is a bay from the Gulf of Alaska and described as Turnagain Arm Inlet. Identified when an English explorer, James Cook in 1778 was forced to turn again when he couldn't find a passage through the mainland to the North west Passage. (An inlet is a channel to the bay).

The Seward Highway is designated as an all-American road and provides spectacular views of the Kenai and Chucach Mountains. Although unfortunately we didn't spot any, Dall sheep and Beluga Whales are occasionally visible. Constant curves slow the speed of larger vehicles, such as "Perser" and for the first time in my many travels I read signs stating: "Pull out for vehicles when more than five vehicles are following".

The opposite side of the road is identified as an avalanche area, and large rocks are deposited on the shoulder. Coupled with high intensity winds buffeting all high-profile means of transport and the wet, slippery, concrete, makes for a memorable driving adventure. These conditions create tense driving, however Nancy as a passenger is able to capture the emotional intensity. I am 100% focused on not toppling into the channel of water.

It was our intention to visit the Crow Creek Historic Goldmine in Gird wood, however the weather was not conducive. Perhaps conditions will improve on our return trip northward.

We failed to see the small sign for our campground on the narrow two-lane road in Moose Pass, which necessitated an additional four miles of travel to find a turn around.

Since arriving in Alaska we have probably read fifty signs alerting us to Moose Crossings and we have only seen four of the massive creatures.

The campground, despite the wet conditions has personality, and site #5 fulfilled our aspirations. It is unfortunate that the rain will prohibit a campfire tonight. We enjoyed a long nap while listening to the raindrops on the metal roof: Very peaceful and relaxing. At 7:00 p.m. I poured my scotch to wash down Nancy's homemade chili. Hopefully morning will bring sunshine for our tourist day in Seward.

Oh, by the way, score is Nancy 30 and Jim 29. We are improving as we average one mental lapse each per day.

DAY #30

Moose Pass continues to reject the sun and the heavy overcast coupled with temperature in the fifties is not inviting. Being as I am a week behind in my scribbling, we elected to stay put and keep pace with our priorities. We aspire to preserve each experience of the "bucket list" adventure in our memories by this written transcript. We can re-live each day by perusal of these words at our leisure for the remainder of our lives.

My writing was interrupted by two naps, which refreshed my mental agility. Nancy engaged in the selection process of retaining and discarding the hundreds of photos thus far. We re-fueled once again on Nancy's pre-trip prepared Meal and retired at 9:00 p.m. Tomorrow we intend to visit the attractions in Seward, regardless of the weather conditions. That is why we travel with umbrellas and rain suits.

DAY # 31

Highlighting the 28-mile drive this morning was the dynamite blasting on Route #9. We were delayed by a flagman while hearing the exploding rocks tumbling down the mountainside. The conspicuous signage alerted motorists to avalanche area and netting to protect the highway was being utilized. We were both impacted by the massive undertaking and 40-minutes hence we're eating our cheerios breakfast in the parking lot at the Seward Visitor Center. The rain has finally ceased following a slippery highway drive.

The ingress to Seward delivered the picture I had envisioned for Alaska towns: Having been acutely disappointed when approaching Fairbanks and Anchorage. The city resides on Resurrection Bay. The engrossing designation was characterized by the retreat of Alexander Baranov in 1792 when he took shelter from a storm on Easter Sunday. The bay is perched on the Kenai Peninsula. The snow-capped mountains emerging from the Chugach National Forest are stunningly visible, situated on the Kenai Fjords the boat harbor is permeated with small and large fishing boats. This endeavor is a primary monetary resource for this charming habitat. (A fjord is a long, narrow, and deep inlet of water that extends far inland and is surrounded by steep cliffs or mountains on three sides). Without difficulty we located an RV parking space on the turquoise water to relax and "take-in" this unique environment (the absence of cruise line vessels was deeply appreciated as those commercial enterprises "lay waste" to charm).

When the visitor's center opened at 9:00 a.m., we gathered all the literature of interest in order to plan our day. While there we engaged in conversation with a couple from Idaho. They were both affable and had chosen to fly to Fairbanks and rent a car. He offered that she preferred to drive; however he was a "scaredy-cat". They quizzed us on our trip and expressed admiration. Had we told them our ages, I suspect they would have been overjoyed for us. During the journey, thus far, we have only engaged in conversation with six couples. I am surprised that probably only half of the seniors are interested in conversing. It may be a symptom of our change in culture that even mature adults are leery of strangers. A change that severely disappoints me.

Our initial visit was the aged railroad station, which has been converted to a cafe. Second was the Alaska Sea Life Center. Although the $35 entrance fee was distressing, our positive anticipation prevailed. The result once again generated a positive value. The array of sea living creatures was amazing, coupled by the very informative displays was over-whelming. It would require a full day to read all the particulars provided.

I was outfitted with a hooded sweatshirt portraying Pittsburgh, PA sports teams that my daughter had pre-sented to me a few years earlier. Two young, attractive female employees spied the shirt and announced their cognition. It was their hometown and they relocated to Seward for the experience. I asked them if they ex-pected to find the love of their life (my oversight) in Seward and they chuckled as they replied, "we already have found it". I was more than a little sheepish as I immediately applauded their blessing. (You some-times cannot judge a book by its cover, and l should know better). Prior to departing we observed an enor-mous sized seal being fed by hand. I didn't realize that seals could grow to that bulk.

A short drive from town conveyed us to the home of 55 Alaskan huskie sled dogs. The cost at $90 each injured my middle-class wallet, however it was sec-ond priority on our adventure. (The first was negated by the fire in Denali). Our two-hour visit commenced by meeting over fifty very enthusiastic Iditarod partic-ipants. The Seavey Homestead lived up to my expec-tations. Including puppies to cuddle, all the huskies were anxious to meet us. Barking with exploding en-ergy while chained to their individual homes, we were stunned by the scene. The method of confinement did disturb me, however it didn't appear to make the canines unhappy. Training the puppies begins while they are very young, by climbing over fallen tree limbs. Although closely related to family pets, their behavior and orientation is vastly different. Even the elderly, over age nine, who do not participate in the race at that age, exhibited a desire to run.

The young man who greeted us upon arrival introduced the dogs by name. It was apparent that he had a "personal" relationship with each member of his "adopted family" Responding to my questions he related that his hometown was Carmichaels, Pennsylvania: population 409. My grandparents played bingo in that town every Saturday night and I joined them on summer vacations: small world. Upon further inquiry he responded: "As a youngster I read about sled dogs and decided I wanted to live that life". He arrived in his elected life two years ago, after attending Edinboro College near Meadville, PA. I am very familiar with that campus as I drove my children's aunt to school many times on snow drifted highways. He demonstrated the use of the dog racing equipment and provided interesting details about the race. The retired dog, Gracie, he utilized to dress in her racing harness and protective garments didn't exhibit pleasure with her selection to participate.

We then boarded a dog sled, which was a metal cart with a capacity of ten. Being as we're the only visitors at that time, the ensuing ride was very personalized. We were guarded on each side with a small chain, while we watched the dogs being selected for our "pull". Every one of the tethered huskies were vigorously appealing for their selection. The musher explained the selective rotation procedure, which obviously wasn't explained to the dogs, as each one thought it should be his or her turn to run. They do get exercised by pulling at a minimum of every other day. Immediately after completing harnessing of the nine dogs we kicked -off with a surge of power. The musher continually uttered directives and motivation, which they didn't appear to need, as Nancy and I scrambled to find a solid location to grasp. We both were expecting a mild speed "take-off", and were "ill-prepared" for the launch. We entered the woods on a very rough and bumpy dirt road as the musher issued commands at each fork. Each change in direction was at full speed and the side chains I deemed inadequate. My left hand grasp remained steadfast and my right hand was gripping Nancy's arm to secure her upright posture: Needless to say it was not what we were expecting, however pleasurably exhilarating. With a full load of passengers, perhaps even children, I don't expect, we would have been treated with this treasurable memory.

The mushers exhibited expertise confirmed the seven Iditarod championships earned by this team.

The eminently trained four legged athletes commence their competition at age two to three years and the female group produces two litters per year to engender the continuity of the team's success. Subsequent to retiring, they are available for adoption and typically live to age 15. Additionally they harbor a team on a glacier to run on their preferred surface and temperature. Visitors are transported by helicopter to participate in the icy experience.

The trailblazer's statue downtown commemorates the history of the Iditarod trail: Recognized as the first ever designated National Historic Trail. In the late 1920's the airplane replaced the contribution of the dog teams.

I do marvel at a very young boy's determination to relocate 5,000 miles to be educated as a musher. It was apparent that he was "living his passion".

Time to refuel at a Safeway grocery.

My intention was to build a roaring campfire tonight, however my energy has eluded me. We both opted for a short nap, however didn't awake until 10:00 p.m. Nancy warmed her most appetizing pork loin and sweet potatoes. I continued my writing until midnight and set the alarm for 5:00 a.m. My phone alerts me to the opening of Denali and that is our first priority destination. Goodnight kiss with Nancy as she munches her salad.

DAY #32

The skies were overcast once again, however the temperature elevated to 55°, and the wind had thankfully vanished. It was striking to see dozens of seaplanes docked on the river, as would typically be boats. A tour guide told us that one in every eighty individuals living in Alaska has an airplane pilot's license. That is hard to accept, although it is obvious by the number of single engine aircraft observed, that it is a popular mode of local transportation. Once more we had hoped to view wildlife on our early morning departure, however that excitement was not in the cards. We encountered severely wavy roads again and were reduced to 40 mph. We found a campground in Cantwell, about 50 miles south of Denali National Park main entrance with electric and water. The parking surface was very large stones and hard on the feet, however campfires to my surprise were permitted. The office receptionist was a very pleasant young woman who moved here from Ocala, Florida. Interestingly probably half the employees in Alaska that I have conversed with are not native. That is a bit of a revelation. She responded; "I am tired of living in flat country."

The environment was not conducive to build a campfire, however I did charcoal grill salmon. Talked with two camper neighbors, one from Canton GA., and the other Spartanburg, S.C.: Both close to our home.

Will set the alarm again tomorrow at 5:00 a.m. Plan to be inside Denali Park before 7:00 a.m. It is scheduled to open at 4:30 a.m. Filled the freshwater tank as not certain where we will sleep tomorrow night.

DAY #33

~ DENALI DAY

V ery big disappointment! We were fourth in line at 6:20 a.m. when we learned that the first available "on and off" bus reservation was at 2:30 p.m. I opted to forego that delay, and Nancy was a bit annoyed with my decision. Two options remained: A narrated bus tour or drive only fifteen miles into the park and return as narration and cost wasn't attractive for me, I chose to drive in. We watched several stop & go buses and Nancy reconsidered her sentiment. When passengers deboarded their only avenue of inspection was hiking trails or bathrooms. I expected great viewing opportunities and they didn't exist. We drove the 30miles in a pretty landscape, although no more spectacular than we have observed since entering the Yukon, and then were told by a "stop everyone" ranger that we could park for an unlimited time period. We enjoyed that view while eating breakfast in "Perser". We watched the "on and off" patrons exercise their disappointment as no wildlife existed. The 30-mile drive plus the 250-mile "backtracking" drive was a complete waste. We did enjoy the exhibits in the Visitors Center.

Prior to the road becoming undriveable, visitors previously drove ninety miles into the park and a RV campground awaited, had that accessibility still existed, I expect my hopeful adventure would have been realized.

While driving to the park, we were shocked to read a large flashing yellow sign "road to Denali Park closed". l informed the attending employee of the incorrect message and he responded "that is a park rangers job". The appropriate response would have been "I will tell the park rangers, thank you". His response exhibits very unsatisfactory employee training.

We departed the park at 10:30 a.m. bound for Glennallen to reside at Ranch House Lodge and RV Camping, which will be a 235 mile jaunt on Route #8. Once in a lifetime is more than enough for this experience, which we would not have had to endure if the Denali fire had not occurred. The highway surface was rolled gravel and oil. Navigation was an average 38.5 MPH for 135 miles, while engaging two flagmen and pilot vehicles. It is apparent that road repairs are constant when the weather permits. The everlasting roughness generated my anxiousness that "Perser" would prevail in this contest. Greatfully, she responded as would a trained sled dog and heeded my commands. The "slow go" yielded a terrific view of snow-covered mountains and a glacier. Off in the distance the Alaska Pipeline dominated the landscape.

Arriving at our campsite at 3:45 p.m., we were delighted to hook- up ten yards adjacent to a rock infested flowing creek. It is a near perfect camping environment with very little wind and temperature in the low sixties. We conversed with our neighbors and joined them in the rustic lodge bar. The female bartender was the owner and talked freely with her six customers at the intimate bar setting. She provided interesting and personal local lure, as we are all beguiled.

The traveler sitting on the bar stool next to me was reared in Steubenville, Ohio. I offered him a family name in that city, and he responded with his relationship to my friend's family: small world.

The total experience was captivating and we opted for a second night at this cache, after touring Valdez tomorrow.

DAY #34

Another early morning as the two to two and a half hour drive each way coupled with sight-seeing will be a full day.

For the first time in a few days we saw a moose crossing the road. Where is all the wildlife in Alaska that I was expecting to see?

The scenery this morning continues to deliver a pleasant drive. Only one flagman today for road improvements. As we dipped into the valleys, dense fog eclipsed our view, however became clear as we spied Worthington Glacier. We were surprised to see a sign directive to a ski slope as gondolas were not in sight.

Twenty-five miles north of Valdez the descent commences to the gorgeous Keystone Canyon with waterfalls racing on both sides of the highway. I read that the Chugach Mountains we just witnessed present nine of the sixteen tallest peaks in the USA. The Lowe River in the canyon reveals strong moving rapids.

The sign declaring the entry of Valdez is fourteen miles prior to the destination. The city doesn't present any charm, however the nearby border of stunning mountains and Prince William Sound fashions a peaceful existence. The Angler's Port harbors hundreds of small trawlers. A solitary prodigious oil tanker dwarfs the fishing endeavor. This vessel portages the discharge from the Alaska Pipeline. Valdez became a household name on March 24, 1989 when the Exxon Corporation agonized with a massive spill.

DAY #35

Today initials one half of our planned bucket list adventure. If the second half rivals the first, we will be exalted by the unparalleled experiences.

We are regretful to bid farewell to our noteworthy campsite on the creek. However, we will be cheerful to "take leave" of the ferocious mosquitos. The repellant was a godsend, as its magic was triumphant.

This sunny travel day necessitates retracing our travel on "Bobber" highway in the opposite direction. I do question my decision to visit Valdez: was the discomforting highway worth the experience? The road surface reminds me of whitewater rafting, as the guide must choose his "steering" very carefully to avoid rocks and precarious currents. The similarity jogs my memory of an indelible occasion on New River Gorge in West Virginia (the newest National Park in the U.S.). Our raft guide announced "watch the guide in the raft ahead of us. He missed the preferred entry channel and the rear of his raft will be lifted out of the water and hurl him forward". As forecast the guide landed on the bow, and only avoided a dip in the rapids as the paid participants grasped the back of his shirt. "Bobber" highway requires total vigilance to avoid the ''foxholes'' and unwanted airtime for "Perser".

The required attentiveness molded a dry mouth and I appealed to Nancy for a peppermint patty from the fridge. Progressing cautiously due to the lurching, she searched in vain proclaiming their absence. I insisted they were on the right side of the small reservoir. With her dander a "weebit" elevated she located them on the left side of the overhead cupboard. Thus, I conceded a point and the score is now Nancy 22, and Jim 21. The flavorful taste did eliminate my irritation.

The tranquility of Kluane Lake on our port side prompted us to reside for the evening at Destruction Bay. (Named for a 1940's severe wind storm) Our first sighting, fortunately was hitherto crammed with half million dollar RV's caravan. The campground only provided electric and possessed zero appeal. Why would the caravan provider choose this uninviting site: perhaps due to an attractive "buyout" cost? As good fortune prevailed once again, only a few miles south we spotted a sign for Cottonwood Park. As we proceeded on the gravel entrance, the proprietor appeared on a golf cart adorned with signage "office". Glenn was very personable and insisted he drive me to inspect all available sites for my selection. The cost was $25, cash, without electric or water, as his generator fuel cost became prohibitive as a result of the COVID ramifications. Our chosen sight on the bay, with ocean-like waves crashing the shoreline, was pristine.

The howling wind prohibits a campfire, however I remain hopeful we can prepare eggs and bacon over the flames in the morning. Having only a three hour drive will issue a leisurely morning.

DAY #36

The wind continued to rock us all night like a baby in the crib. We listened to the bay waves pummel the earth only twenty yards from our domain. The white caps are a stark contrast to the tranquil lakes we have been enjoying for the past three weeks.

In our late eighties we have similarities to our crib age, as we need assistance at times to navigate an uneven surface. Falling at our age could be debilitating and constant caution is a wise commitment: no shame in holding on.

Not being able to cook over the flames, we slept late as we only have a drive of 162 miles to Pioneer

RV Park in Whitehorse, Yukon. Hopefully my requested campsite, #130 on the hill, will be awaiting. On our trip north I was able to saw kindling, and I am in need of that fuel once more.

As we approached Haines Jct., the flavor of those cinnamon rolls at the Village Bakery consumed our senses. A crowd of perhaps thirty customers were having lunch in the small structure, as most were sitting on the outside deck. The peanut butter cookies also looked inviting.

Sadly we caught sight of a wounded and scraggly wolf crossing the road and limped to the shoulder of the surface. One of his or her hind legs was severely limiting progress. No doubt the end is close by as catching prey with limited mobility is unlikely.

We are delighted to hook-up in site #130 once again as I could gather my hidden firewood, set aside on our previous visit. The wind no longer dominated our activities, and at 4:00 p.m. the campfire provided welcoming relaxation. I plan to cut more branches in the morning to load in "Perser's" storage area with all the other outdoor camping supplies including tables and chairs. (A suitable storage area is necessary to provide a satisfactory camping experience) Hopefully border inspections in the time ahead will be lenient, as it was when entering the Yukon on this border crossing.

Our charcoal grilled fish by the flames "hit the spot" given the absence of mosquitos.

DAY #37

A t 7:03 a.m. my feet felt the cool surface of the wood floor, as requisitioned the prior evening. I never cease to be amazed by the synchronization of the mind and body. I ponder the limits of that potentiality if we ever master the connection.

It was a perfect morning for a campfire as I complete my kindling cutting: no wind and sweatshirt temperature. We ravaged the tantalizing cinnamon rolls while I finished my daily record of our experiences.

As we move south on Rte. #2, I look forward to retrieving my Verizon cell phone service in Alaska: I miss my news and emails.

Strong crosswinds again prompt me to drive in the center of the highway when possible. Thankfully we have a smooth surface to traverse: absence of permafrost aftermath. Hooray we sight a caribou crossing ahead of us and walking briskly into the trees. We are constantly on the lookout for the "northland" wildlife.

The Alaska border inspection was our first interior scrutiny. The man was quite brusque and far less than personable. He searched our fridge for chicken void of an explanation. I don't eat chicken, however that is another story. He then queried me about firewood (initial appeal) and stated "show it to me". I opened the storage area and he confiscated my two hours of cutting. Had I anticipated his action, I could have hidden the cherished possession on the roadside and retrieved on the return excursion.

The landscape shifted dramatically as we passed by beautiful Tinglish Lake. Fog emerged and drops of water engulfed the windshield as the cool air prompted condensation. Suddenly I felt like the "Tinman" walking with Dorothy through the Enchanted Forest. Slightly visible, due to the fog, large rocks burst out of the earth covered with "moss like", only taller, vegetation. Severely twisted four to six foot high willowy trees with virtually no leaves protruded from the adjourning bedrock. The scene was "eerie" and surreal, and unfortunately brief. It created the feeling of a vision.

Fourteen miles prior to entering Skagway we commenced a lengthy descent to sea level, with multiple switch backs requiring little opportunity for the driver to take pleasure in the landscape. I did spot a sign announcing "land of the northwind". I concurred when arriving at the campsite, and had to struggle to maintain my balance. Experiencing total dissatisfaction with the very open, no trees, crowded spaces at the Garden City RV Park, I immediately decided to search for a more comfortable campground. (Box of chocolates) Perhaps one night would have been tolerable, however planning to remain for three nights in this "hamlet" was objectionable. We were able to upgrade from $50 per night to $75 per night at Pullen Creek Campground. Since both locations are city owned, a refund was not necessary. Pullen Creek was tolerable, however not enticing. The weather forecast is rain with potential flooding. "Perser" may provide our only comfort. The site did not even provide a picnic table and campfires were not permitted. It was necessary to bungy cord the electric plug to connect it, as the base was in disrepair. (If you are reading this as a guide to future travel, I suggest you research another location. Perhaps the National Park Service DYEA Campground, nine miles from Skagway, would be a superior choice)

An inspection at the visitor's center provided an employee's recommendation to attend a musical production of the gold rush. When we arrived at the scheduled 2:30 p.m. performance the door was locked, despite a conspicuous sign stating "daily operation".

The probably one hundred downtown buildings are 1800's appearing and generate the feel of the period. In stark contrast, two cruise vessels are docked in the harbor. Only a very few tourists are braving the weather as the wooden plank sidewalks are nearly barren.

Skagway was originally named "Shgaggwei", which in Tlingit translates to "bunched up water". It was Alaska's first incorporated and gateway to the Klondike Gold Rush in 1898. Year-round residents total about 1,000 and is the northernmost point of the inside passage. The intended miners seeking their fortune, supported more than eight saloons. A replica of the Red Onion dance hall and bordello includes a museum.

DAY #38

The downtown streets this morning are an over-flow of cruise passengers. (J found the city considerably more attractive yesterday) It has the feel of a carnival crowd (cruise line). Dodging umbrellas on the boardwalk was annoying as the passengers were oblivious to their disconcerting behavior.

Successfully ventured to the "Days Of 98 Show" once again for the 10:30 a.m. performance. When asking I was informed that yesterday's performance was cancelled due to the absence of cruise tourists. Too bad the visitor's center wasn't informed, or the door sign changed. One on stage performer advertised that venue by hanging one tantalizing leg outside the second floor window and vocalizing her appeal for attendance. The dancers and skit were assuredly entertaining, and introduced us to the real life character of "Soapy Smith". Before arriving in Skagway in 1897, he had been booted out of Denver owing to his con man activities peddling soap. Soon after establishing residence he joined forces with a reverend, and they assembled the largest band of thieves in North America. During his nine months of reign he cultivated the persona of an upstanding philanthropist and was chosen as Grand Master of the July 4 parade, riding his white horse. (Reminds me of the Marfia organization in the 1940's) Four days later he robbed a miner (stampeder) of $2,800 in gold dust, resulting in a gun fight to his demise.

In 1923 passenger steamships started ushering tourists to this historic gold rush locale. In an effort to raise money for the Skagway hockey team, this show was contrived, and has become the long running tradition from that time forward.

The combination of persistent rain and tourist's umbrellas prompted our return to "Perser" for the remainder of the day.

DAY #39

Today we visit the capital of Alaska, Juneau by boat. It is astonishing that a capital city cannot be reached by highway travel. That decision was reached in 1906 due to population growth generated by the gold mining industry. The previous capital was Sitka. The unlikely capital location was purchased from Russia in 1867 and was Alaska's first city.

Locating the docked catamaran pontoon was a challenge in the rain. Despite having received an email path, it required three attempts to initiate the waiting line at 7:15 a.m. The frustration elevated when instructed to scale a two-foot-high rope on the dock. (Stainless steel knees) While scrambling, a French Canadian couple, in line to our rear, raced by us to be seated at their inclination. My immediate impulse to verbally admonish their rudeness was stifled by the realization that Nancy would be embarrassed by my initiative. We would be mingling with one hundred other tourists on this excursion for twelve hours. The couple, in their fifties, continued to bolt to the front the remainder of the day. Too often human nature is revealed as ugly.

The speedy vessel navigated the Gastineau Channel and Tracy Arm with the young shipmaster making the decisions. He appeared to be a teenager, however, revealed age twenty-five when asked. His female assistant was overtly gracious with a beckoning smile as she served a most welcome cup of coffee. Her demeanor kindled an appreciation of our choice to choose "FJORD EXPRESS TO JUNEAU". I have high regard for staff who exhibit respect for $189 each expenditure.

In contrast to the ill-mannered Canadians, a single man in his forties offered assistance to Nancy as she walked to the restroom on the rocking vessel. Later in the day he also saved us a front row seat on the bus and then retreated to the rear. (The Canadians sat across the aisle in the front row behind the driver)

The magnificent bordering mountains were partially eclipsed by the stagnant fog, which created a pleasing glide on the water. Waterfalls and glaciers, as well as an eagle breakfasting on a fish, came into view. We docked in Haines to gather more passengers for the Alaska Marine Highway. Haines is connected to the Yukon by the Alaska Highway. Another eagle was perched on the dock post. Sea lions were relaxing on the large rocks emerging from the FJORD. Nancy was busy photographing the abundance of wildlife.

The young ship captain had been surveying these waters since a youngster with his father, who previously led this tour. He was extremely knowledgeable and narrated all points of interest, including the three lighthouses. The ultimate joy for all voyagers occurred as we entered North Pass. Dozens of small commercial boats, similar to our transportation, were stationary as their passengers peered over the rail into the "deep blue sea". At a distance spewing mammals were feeding incessantly. Their tails emerged frequently to the delight of all observers. The whales endure this nourishing habitat for the duration of summer and then swim south to "fast" all winter.

The approach to Juneau was dispiriting as large cruise ships dominated the setting: no charm. The bus driver narrated our trip to downtown and it was apparent he enjoyed his labor. Glad it isn't raining in Juneau, after constant rain in Skagway.

Larry, the RV caravan director I conversed with while camping weeks ago, had suggested Tracys for a crab lunch. We opted for crab cakes as the crab legs were $55. Seating was family style and we shared tales. The taste of crab was pleasing and we then perched on a downtown park bench as the scores of cruisers passed by. People watching is entertaining. Sea planes taking off to the glacier with tourists provided additional amusement. Their revenue affords Juneau a plentiful bounty.

The 4.5 hour return trip was less exciting as it was a rerun. Although Juneau was a big disappointment, I felt visiting the capital of Alaska was a fore-most experience on this journey. The boat ride provided a good value for our expense. Being sixteen hours since the alarm beckoned, I was quite weary and "hit the sack" soon after climbing into "Perser"

DAY #40

It is raining again this early morning, fourth consecutive day, as we travel to depart our adventure in Alaska. Our yen was satisfied, and yet we sense dismay to enter the return trip home. We could have easily relished another two weeks in this scenic landscape. If I were replanning, I would drive further south on Rte. #1 after leaving Seward to Kenai and Homer. I would eliminate the trek to Valdez, however that is only a personal preference. The campgrounds we found most appeasing, I would "hang out" another day or two. However, that would have required changing all reservations: not a welcome task. At a younger age I would certainly consider more camping in the Yukon and Alaska. I would not revisit the cruise invested major urban areas, although glad I toured their attractions. Without a doubt we are blessed at our age to have made this journey.

The drive north from Skagway, despite the drizzle and overcast skies is magnificent. We climb for eleven miles to a n elevation of 3,292 feet, having camped at 35 feet. The Canadian customs agent was very personable and did not require an inspection of "Perser's" interior.

We have decided to deviate from the planned route as auxiliary voyagers suggested we utilize Rte. #37 tomorrow to witness the bear population. While traversing Rte. #8 east we did observe one young black bear moving west on the shoulder of the road. He or she had an undisclosed destination as due we for tonight's campsite. The subsequent 321 miles revealed Baby Nugget RV Park in Watson Lake on the Alaska Highway. $60, cash only, included electric and water in a sparsely treed setting: personally rated as satisfactory. The rain has ceased and a light breeze prevails, which permits a campfire. However, I feel my second head cold approaching and elect to rest rather than grill outdoors. Nancy serves more home-made soup.

DAY #41

D riving Rte. #37 south was disappointing as only one bear was spotted. Nancy observed it darting into the forested landscape, and I missed the sighting. Observing these massive, yet speedy, strong brutes was a journey priority for me as I expected to see numerous each day during this adventure. (Including city streets)

The 488 mile trip today was rather humdrum, if you can consider the majestic landscape with that label. We have been treated to that experience for 25 consecutive days. How quickly one can get spoiled. No wind and no rain with only two road construction delays totaling about 30 minutes.

My head cold required a forty-five-minute nap before continuing to Ksan RV Park in Hazelton, British Columbia. The campsite was excellent, being on the creek with good grass.

DAY #42

Driving to Prince George, B.C. was good highway and easy driving until we reached rain for the last two hours. We witnessed two dangerous drivers who passed in a passing lane and then abruptly pulled in front of us when the lane ended, causing me to hit the breaks on the wet slippery road surface.

A couple of miles after leaving Ksan Campground we traversed a one lane, very narrow bridge which only permitted one truck at a time to cross.

We saw our first deer of the nearly nine thousand miles travelled. As we approach Smither, B.C. the landscape changes dramatically. This location could easily be mistaken for Franklin, N.C.: looking at the Blue Ridge and Smoky Mountain ranges, large fields of freshly mowed hay capture the eye. We have reentered the domesticated world, although moose warnings still exist, unlike Franklin. The highway traffic becomes light after numerous days of near total isolation.

Approximately ninety miles west of Prince George we were delighted to spot a black bear. He or she was travelling west and us east, thus unable to capture a photo. We also had a good look at a large deer with velvet covered antlers on his big rack.

We had to hook-up at campground in the rain. The site assigned by the office staff was already occupied: just what I need after an eight hour day nursing my cold: rain and ineffective management. (Box of chocolates) The young man phoned his boss and said eight times (I counted them) "he says #23 has an RV on it, but #25 is open". He told me he is the maintenance man and doesn't like being summoned for office work. His mother-in-law owns the campground and he has no recourse to her directives.

Set the alarm for 7:00 a.m. as the plan is to drive 277 miles tomorrow, our final day in Canada.

DAY #43

Bright sunshine quickly turned to light fog as the fifty-nine degrees dropped to fifty-two degrees. Shortly after passing through Quesnel, a charming small town, saw a big rack on a tall deer. While stopped for breakfast, I checked the tires and found one worn badly on the inside: not visible on the outside. We stopped at the first tire company and replaced both front tires. Feel more comfortable now, however Nancy's comfort is in peril as she remains in bed with my head cold.

I was delighted to see a small black bear, not much bigger than a cub, cross the highway and jaunt up a driveway in a residential area. This is what I expected to experience in Alaska multiple times but did not.

Wildfire warning being posted and I can see and smell the heavy smoke. Now I can actually see the fire coming from the other side of the wooded mountain. The side roads are closed and blocked by emergency vehicles: shocked to see 112 degrees temperature on my dash.

As the landscape changed dramatically once again, from farming acreage to enormous height mountains, the scene developed as an under the Christmas tree decoration. The gorge several thousand feet below envelopes a large river with fast moving rapids. On both sides of the river trains travel in opposite directions, with mountains bordering both sets of tracks. The highway, Rte.#16, is very narrow with hairpin curves and although I preferred to watch the scene below more closely, the priority is to safely steer "Perser" to the bottom. Unfortunately there were no "turnouts" to park and engulf the magical experience. It would be a delight to have that experience often, while I realize it is a once in a lifetime opportunity. Those mountains reached as high as the eye could see, about seventy miles north of Hope, B.C. on Rte. #1.

Drove 414 miles today.

DAY #44

Coquihalla Campground in Hope, B.C. sits on the creek by the same name. The sites have just enough trees to provide a feeling of privacy. The creek has a swimming "hole", as did my Conoquenessing Creek in Ellwood City, PA. where I was raised. Our "hole" was named "Sunshine", and had a rope tied to a tree for swinging to let go and splash into the "hole". A bit dangerous as timing to release the grip on the rope, could mean dropping into huge boulders.

Nancy is feeling improved this morning.

Vancouver, B.C. at 8:00 a.m. is an interesting drive, although challenging. Somehow we lost Rte. #99 through the downtown and eventually found Rte. 99A through the suburbs of Center City for about an hour. We viewed considerably more than intended. I expected to sail through the city on a Sunday morning, however the highway traffic was at times gridlocked. Crossing the U.S. Border was considerably different than all previous border experiences. Probably one hundred vehicles lined up to report to seven inspectors. Our young man was very congenial and did ask if he could inspect our cooler. What would have happened if I had said no? Nothing good I would imagine! Total time at the border was about thirty minutes.

Off we go to probably our last lifetime reentry to our home country. Looks like the universe is going to permit our back bumper Wyoming driftwood to re-side in Franklin. Nary an inspector noticed the large object wrapped in a blue tarp: we got lucky!

At 11:30 a.m. we encountered the first prolonged gridlock of this journey and the discomfort remained all driving day. Having anticipated a seven hour day, it required ten hours for the 406 miles. We witnessed the remnants of only our second accident: pleased, how-ever surprised by the dearth. Motoring on Interstate #5 in the state of Washington is similar in traffic conges-tion to Interstate #95 in Florida. We covered 406 miles today, before arriving at Paradise Point State Park in Ridgefield, Washington. I rated the campsite as poor with highway noise and lack of privacy.

DAY #45

At precisely 11:30 a.m. Nancy was introduced to the Pacific Ocean in Lincoln City, Oregon. At that juncture we commenced travel on the Pacific Coast Highway, Rte. #101. Being my first vis-it to Oregon, I was unaware that the awesome ocean views rival that of California. The remaining day's drive through small charming towns was delightful.

About 5:00 p.m. we were overjoyed as we pulled into Site #8, at Alfred Loeb State Park in Brooking, Oregon. We are enclosed with large trees which be-stows privacy on a spacious lot. Dined on charcoal grilled burgers with all the fixings including grilled mushrooms. The campfire accommodated a perfect camping experience. A short walk to view the creek erased a few calories. (We should walk more often) When we returned to the glowing ashes, we were absorbed by a very large beautiful blue bird: the likes of which neither of us have ever beheld. Too bad Nancy was unable to photograph, as she was engaged in feeding our visitor bread, before he or she vanished.

Today was an excellent new adventure day.

DAY #46

The big, beautiful bird returned to our campsite this early morning as I was drinking coffee by the campfire and writing: no doubt anticipating another feeding. Receiving only disappointment, its wings unfurled and disappeared into the bright sunshine.

"In what state is your motorhome registered?" The California state inspector checked her literature and then issued a directive for a Gypsy Moth examination. Her words were a shock to my A-FIB irregular heartbeat. When queried she replied "worst case you will receive a free high-pressure wash if we find evidence of that pest" My non-disclosed immediate concern was our blue tarped keepsake. Would we be commanded to disrobe the back bumper? The "microscopic" procedure endured for one hour as an unidentified "blob" was discovered. It was extracted to the lab for a judgement, thus the extended delay. The "blob" remained a mystery and the wash conducted, only requiring ten minutes. Why the microscope rather than just do the wash and save me fifty minutes of delay? There was not a solitary question about the blue overwrap and it could have been concealing any nuisance. A testament to the reputation of California's elevated cost of living and overkill. The young woman conveying the explanation was especially pleasant and apologized for the lengthy delay.

The Gypsy Moth, during the caterpillar stage, eats as much as a square foot of leaves daily and is capable of defoliating trees. Each egg mass contains up to 1,000 eggs, and are laid between July and September. The pest was brought to New England from Europe in 1869 by a naturalist looking for a way to develop a disease-resistant silkworm. A windstorm blew the cage door open and the ravagers propagated. They have no naturally occurring enemies in the United States. North Carolina is as far south as they inhabit, and west to Illinois, as related by our congenial examiner.

Our reservation in Trinidad, California at Suemeg State Park did not include electric or water, as these luxuries do not exist. Despite the boondocking inconvenience the experience was rated excellent. (Box of chocolates) Giant redwood trees engulfed our campsite and the red flame roasted hot dogs were inviting: just a delightful evening. Going to retire early as we will be driving through the Redwood Forest early in the morning before sightseeing in San Francisco.

DAY #47

When as a ten year old, my father drove my mother and I to California. I vividly recall the huge tree with a hole to drive cars through. Of course that isn't possible with "Perser". However, did get a photograph of a red sports car convertible "taking the plunge". The $15 cost was reasonable: wish I could remember the cost in 1947.

San Francisco traffic was less congested than expected. The sloped streets that characterize the city in the movies was a confirmation to Nancy of the "taking air" by chasing vehicles. The bicyclists were flooding the Golden Gate Bridge as we crossed and had a good view of Alcatraz (named by a Spanish explorer in 1775)

After a long day of adventure, we began our search for Henry Cowell Redwoods State Park in Felton, California. The park was exactly where the global positioning system said it would be, however the campground at 8:00 p.m. was unrevealed. The entrance kiosk was unmanned at that hour, and we made four or five U-turns in our search. Resorting to further delays, we questioned store clerks and walkers to little avail. After four inquiries we found an individual who was familiar with the location. It was five miles down the highway from the park entrance. At 9:00 p.m., tired and hungry, we arrived at Site #32, only to discover a pickup truck resting in the site. I carried my golf club into the darkness, not knowing what type of individual I might encounter. He was sitting in a fold-up chair and perusing his cell phone. He was middle aged and politely responded "I will get out of your way". Arriving late to a campground is never a good idea!

Our fifteen hour day was a bit exhausting, and I was more than ready to feel the comfort of the mattress. I wonder if my old bones will feel rested in the morning. As I age, increased rest time is needed to recover from exertion. A seven to eight hour, on the road, day has not been tiring.

DAY #48

The morning sunlight revealed an excellent boondocking campsite with firepit. My bones were rejuvenated and energy restored sufficiently to erect the kindling branches.

When exiting the campground at 9:10 a.m. we spotted the white pickup truck scavenger parked in a campsite. "I see you found another site to sleep", I shouted out the open window. Having pulled in I could view his license plate number and l read it loudly, making certain he could hear me. Sitting again in his chair, he did not exhibit any concern or aggravation. I drove to the park office to alert them to the obviously unregistered guest, however it was closed. (Box of chocolates)

Startling how the landscape changes from day to day, and somedays from hour to hour. The agricultural fields are pervaded with "pickers" laboring to feed their families. It is humbling to realize the gift of birth. That could have been me toiling to maintain the only lifestyle obtainable. The irrigation sprinklers are also providing their contribution to production.

We exited the highway to take a driving tour of Monterey and marveled at the Spanish architecture.

Paid the $12 entrance fee to delight in the opulence bordering the celebrated SEVENTEEN MILE DRIVE. (Pickers and mansions only separated by a few miles) The PGA golf courses fronting the ocean are manicured to perfection. We visited the Poppy Hills Golf Course pro shop as it is one of the few public links in the Del Monte Forest locale. We reveled when entering Crocker Grove, home to the largest and oldest Monterey cypress trees in existence. A strong ocean breeze compliments the colliding waves generated by submerged rocks, while the visible rocks are refuge for sunbathing harbor seals and barking sea lions. The experience is capped with a visit to the Pebble Beach Visitor Center, which provides a history of the 1800's carriage ride. In my million plus driving miles in the U.S., and a few thousand more by air and sea to Europe, South America, and the Far East, I deem this parcel of earth "one of a kind". The pristine nature has been augmented by gifted development.

Once again exited the thoroughfare to visit the charming streets of Carmel. Once wasn't sufficient to satisfy our thirst, thus we repeated our course to "gulp in" the flavor.

On to San Simeon State Park in Cambria, California where there was not a tree in sight. The site had zero privacy and we rated as poor. We travelled 315 miles today.

DAY #49

Big day as we will tour the Hearst Castle at 9:40 a.m.

Arrived at the parking lot at 8:30 a.m. and it was difficult to locate handicap parking.

The bus embarks at the visitor's center without notification for a fifteen minute ride up the steep mountain. We sat in the front seat and could enjoy the switch back turns void of guard rails. The castle came into view as we climbed and appeared majestic. We engaged in joviality with one senior couple and were excited for the adventure.

The walking tour was arduous, however the temperature remained in the seventies and sitting benches and water fountains were frequently available. The castle is really a complex of buildings and sculptures and architectural wonderment. William Randolph Hurst liked to entertain guests, which he did often, and horseback riding was his favorite endeavor. His taste for European deco was formulated at age ten when visiting the "old country" with his mother. Following the tour we watched the movie describing his childhood and love to be a "builder".

After three nights of boondocking, looking forward to recharging which electricity and water. The Ventura Beach Resort at $143 per night provides full hook-up and a swimming pool and hot tub. The cost is prohibitive, however, no other campgrounds are available. What a disappointment and rip-off: overpriced! No trees, no grass, no privacy, difficult back in, and not even a picnic table. The scene was kids, bicycles, pets, and vehicles lining the driveways. While hooking-up was compelled to side step the previous camper's dog poop.

DAY #50

Took advantage of the only appreciated luxury: the early morning hot tub. On the way out left a written message for the owner stating my below standard rating, and requesting a refund: no response was received.

While driving south on 1-405 witnessed multiple motorcyclists weaving lanes at probably 80 MPH plus. The anticipated Los Angeles gridlock required eighty minutes to conquer. After exiting at Laguna Beach we crawled for another hour to Rte. #1 and the beach. That throughway was a sea of humanity, and parking space did not exist. However the sluggish movement provided ample opportunity to gaze at the beach revelers, as well as the relaxing sunbathers. Upscale retailers occupy every space available.

Once again campgrounds were filled to capacity, and had been since my early attempts for reservations in February. We located a parking spot, after several pass throughs in a lot on the beach at Dana Point. Napping to the sound of the crashing waves was a special treat. The swimmers and surfers began exiting about 6:00 p.m., and the sunset onlookers arrived at dusk. We placed our chairs earlier to save a space.

Free boondocking on the beach seemed too good to be awarded and it was. As we slept soundly, a robust knock on the door awakened us at 10:30 p.m. "This parking lot closes at 10:00 p.m.", was the proclamation. After being rousted for the initial time on this glorious travel, we drove only five miles down the main street and parked: slept soundly the remainder of the night.

DAY #51

At 6:00 a.m. I returned to the Dana Point Beach, and placed our chairs on the sand for the morning experience. I had exhausted my first cup of coffee when Nancy decided to join in the adventure at 7:30 a.m. The crashing waves continued to captivate all of our senses. Want to "take it all in" as it no doubt will be our final viewing of the Pacific

Ocean uniqueness. We walked to the beach and put our feet in the cool water. The early morning surfers were dressing in their wet suits preparing for their regular exercise. I observed one paddle board with a propeller and steering mechanism. It had good speed and provided the opportunity for the sole occupant to "take air" in the waves and then dive losing total power: First time I have seen that toy.

Mid-afternoon we camped at San Clemente Beach State Parle, the site once again has no trees, however affords minimum privacy and a campfire ring. Four months ago when I made the reservation electric and water were not available: only a handicap site which is adjacent to the rest rooms and showers with constant foot traffic alongside our residence. We charcoal grilled excellent salmon. Surprised to discover the television will not operate: probably too much rough road.

DAY #52

Abandoned the campsite at 7:00 a.m. to complete a driving tour of San Diego this morning. The tour was all I had hoped for. Surprisingly we encountered no traffic during the morning rush hour. Initially entered the harbor marina and watched the morning boats going fishing at 8:30 a.m., while we ate breakfast in "Perser": nice experience. We drove through downtown and were impressed with the city view. Having spent time here thirty years ago, while in the corporate world, I always found it to be a most comfortable surrounding. Constant ocean cool breeze, moderate temperatures year round, no icy winter, mountains within a forty five minute drive and a beautiful boat harbor. I was surprised and delighted to see the Midway Navy aircraft carrier docked in the harbor and the home of numerous aircraft, now a museum. While in the Marine Corps I resided on that famous ship while the pilots were making practice landings at sea. I witnessed two planes, pilots enclosed, miss their landing approaches and disappear into the ocean: a daunting experience.

We drove to Coranado Island over a very high bridge yielding a n excellent view of the harbor and the hundreds of docked and moored vessels of all types and sizes.

I wanted Nancy to get a glimpse of the hotel Del Coranado, which she did. It is famous for the multiple roof lines and has been utilized in many Hollywood films.

We are now driving to the desert and forecasted temperatures in the 100's-ow! Desert Trails RV Park and Golf Course, here we come, in El Centro, California.

DAY #53

The air conditioner in "Perser" was activated all night, and it remained uncomfortable to sleep. Leaving at 6:30 a.m. the temperature registers one hundred degrees. In Gila Bend, Arizona I was shocked to see a Calgon Carbon Company regeneration facility. I worked as a chemical technical representative for that company at their home office in Pittsburgh, Pennsylvania.

Nancy lost a point as she neglected to turn off the ignition switch last evening when installing the front windshield cover. Thankfully I noticed the dash lights on before retiring. Checked the start-up and all is okay. Score in game is Nancy 27 and Jim 26, however keep in mind Nancy is the scorekeeper. Jim lost his last point for forgetting to lock the door when exiting to pump gas. We are alert to car-jacking.

We encountered a fifty-five minute gridlock traffic delay due to road construction just an hour prior to reaching our campground. Longest delay to date.

Rock Hound State Park in Deming, New Mexico offered mostly open sites, as was ours, however the distance between did provide satisfactory privacy. The picnic tables are located within a concrete structure which is atypical and inviting. However, the swarm of flies prohibits any outdoor activities. Why don't they spray to eliminate the intruders? We are now in the Chihuahuan Desert and only thirty-three miles north of the Mexican border.

DAY #54

E ven at 7:00 a.m. the flies exercise their control over tranquility. After one hour on the highway we crossed the Rio Grande River at Las Cruces. Observing the water ignites my reminiscence of the many western movies wherein the "bad guys" flee the chasing marshals.

A border patrol inspection by sniffing German Shepards transpired in fleeting moments, unlike the inspection in California.

Having gained a day on our planned schedule, due to undesirable campgrounds, I phoned Bottomless State Park in Roswell, New Mexico in an attempt to arrange early arrival. However, was frustrated by a message "mailbox full cannot accept messages". We decided to risk the twelve mile, off our primary Rte. #70, jaunt in hopes for an available site. The frustration elevated when we determined the office was unstaffed. Once locating the camp host's site, knocked on the RV door and met a receptive man in his sixties. He related that his wife, who carries the computer, was shopping in town and he didn't know if any sites were available. Having driven through the campground to find his whereabouts, I observed it was sparsely populated. I asked if he could phone his wife to assign us a site. Why didn't he offer to take that action? (Box of chocolates) Standing in the sun parched desert in one hundred and four degrees to accomplish what should have been an unnecessary task was "boiling" activity.

Apparently his as well.

Once again early to bed and will unhook early in the morning before the sun melts the water hose (Ha-Ha) and drive to the widely known UFO Region. Perhaps there will be a museum of interest to explore visitors from outer space (Ha-Ha)

DAY #55

The city is 1a dichotomy of appealing Spanish architecture and repetitive commercial franchise structures. It was very disheartening to realize the "landing site" is on private property, twenty miles distant from town and not approachable. Signage throughout the locale does lay claim to the unexplained Incident. It is personally perplexing, and I wonder if the government will ever be able to reveal its nature. No doubt, the disclosure might be frightening.

The only noteworthy sights during today's motoring are the slaughter house stockyards: many thousands of cattle are bunched together in mud laden pens. They appear drastically uncomfortable and distraught. Hopefully my impression is inappropriate given their feeble cerebral matter.

At 4:30 p.m. "Perser" was parked on tranquil Lake Foss in Oklahoma. The site is lined with trees and provides "backyard" privacy. Nancy would have indulged the warm water had the 107-degree temperature not been prohibitive. We were relegated to the view beyond our windshield, as the air conditioner provided comfort. We have been travelling now for four days in oppressive heat. Looking forward to the relief as we leave the west. We piloted 405 miles today.

DAY #56

Oklahoma boasts high winds and damaging tornadoes, and we endured those vehicle rocking vibrations most of the night. The good news is those winds ushered in a break in the heat wave. A pleasant seventy-five degrees at 7:00 a.m. permitted coffee and breakfast beside the "still waters". The relief is graciously appreciated.

Leaving the desolate landscape we are proceeding at 70 MPH on cruise control. The topography now rivals Pennsylvania where Nancy and I both were reared by attentive and loving parents. (I volunteer as a Guardian Ad Litem, to provide counsel and leadership to those youngsters not as fortunate as we were).

We observe two cars being fixed upon a wrecker, and count our blessings to have avoided a similar fate. 1-40 led us through Okla homa City void of gridlock. I have toured that city previously and unearthed a trove of cowboy history.

Camped on Lake Darnelle in Russellville, Arkansas at 4:00 p.m. We have availed ourselves of this pleasant surrounding in the past, however our preferred site on the water with deck, was not available when making reservations. Not as fortunate this visit as the field of vision was rusted metal roof on the boat house. Unfortunate we could not book site #4.

DAY #57

The weather this morning is conducive for outside residing, however we need to put the rubber to the concrete as we are scheduled to meet with Nancy's relative near Memphis.

The two semi's transporting cattle generated a chuckle as their dangling cowbells jiggled from the rear bumper.

We "got cracking" after the refreshing visit for T.O. Fuller State Park. As is our customary practice, we followed the roadside brown signs to lead us to our destination. We were shocked to be halted by a closed road: new bridge being constructed. We employed Waze GPS to yield a solution and "she" did so successfully. One half hour later I questioned the office attendant who replied "we have requested that those signs be removed and replaced, however to no avail": shame on the state of Tennessee.

For the first evening in five days we sat by the campfire as I sipped scotch.

DAY #58

W hen we purchased "Perser" we were issued a free week of camping by a company with intentions to sell us a membership. One of their listed locations is in eastern Ohio and is described as a horse ranch. Appealing to my taste, we have elected to exploit the offer. Nancy also rides horseback, however has not had the opportunity in many years. I developed my riding enthusiasm when my daughter was a teenager and my initial endeavor occurred in the mountains of Colorado. Nancy commenced riding a pony on her family's dairy farm as a youngster.

Rather than "head" south to North Carolina, we will "head" north.

The drive to Lucas, Kentucky "sets the stage" as we pass numerous white fence lined thoroughbred pastures. The four-legged creatures majestically enhance the countryside.

We did observe two more damaged vehicles being lifted to a tow truck. Amazingly this is only the fourth accident sight we have encountered.

Barren River Lake State Park boasts a golf course and swimming. The 293 mile drive was without incident and we rested comfortably by the campfire. We rated the campsite as good.

DAY #59

After scanning the golf course and examining the condition of the greens, I elected to play eighteen holes. It was a favorable decision and Nancy once again delighted in driving the cart. She has learned to no longer drive too close to the greens as the cart monitor terminated forward progress. Initially she had concluded the cart had malfunctioned, and her learning curve was short-lived. We had so much fun we opted to repeat the experience tomorrow.

Another pleasant evening following Nancy's lake plunge. (I have never been an enthusiastic "take a dip" participant).

DAY #60

We will travel 406 miles today, universe willing to the horse ranch. The lady attending the registration post was congenial and courteous. The campground literature was disappointing as it revealed an extremely limited horseback riding schedule. However, the assigned campsite was even more discouraging. I was anticipating a view of horses in the pasture for a week: perhaps even the opportunity to stroke the mane on occasion through the fence rails. To the contrary the location was totally undesirable. Severely sloped, rock infested, and my power cord wasn't sufficiently long to reach the source post. An absolute disaster for a marketing invitation.

The young man on the golf cart leading us was "in tune" to my discomfort and directed our movement to a different undesirable campsite. The only improvement being my power cord length was now tenable.

DAY #61

A t 9:00 a.m. a knock on the door interrupted our cereal breakfast. "They want to see you in the office as you don't belong in this site". The social security eligible employee waited while I prepared for the encounter. During the five minute cart ride we had a pleasant "get to know each other" conversation, primarily relating his life story. (I always enjoy those stories from new acquaintances).

The pleasantness abruptly ended when entering the registration office. An antagonistic demeanor announced "you don't belong there". My rebuttal adopted a similar tone. "I was directed there last evening as my power cord would not reach your post". "We were not told that, who directed you to that campsite?" The inference clearly being that I was telling an untruth. Now I am seriously incensed and feeling insulted replied "it appears I need to contact your home office before initiating a law suit for character assassination".

A female manager apparently overheard the disagreement and interceded. "Sorry for the misunderstanding, we thought you selected that site without permission". "I suggest you train your employees to ascertain the facts prior to making accusations". "The young man who directed you last night is a new employee and did not realize his decision was a mistake". "Paul, please take this gentleman through the campground and have him select any site available".

When returning to the golf cart, Paul offered "she is always unpleasant and I don't know how she keeps her job". I responded: "perhaps she is a relative of management?" (A caramel in a box of chocolates).

As we traversed the grounds I observed the stables, however, no horses. Upon being questioned, Paul responded "we only have four trail horses and they are all in use": another disappointment!

Nary an available site was appealing, and only a very few unavailable locations as well. I settled on one up the mountain, not being certain I could navigate the terrain in "Perser". It did provide a little privacy with trees and a campfire location. However, it required backing in a length of perhaps one hundred yards through trees that required numerous steering wheel rotations. I conditioned my selection based on accomplishment. Paul remained to determine my success or failure. Succeeding, I needed to return to the office on the golf cart to confirm my site selection. During this visit the offensive employee's demeanor transformed to congenial. We concluded our dialog without any further aggravation. "To say the least", it was not the manner in which I expected to start the day. After relating the discomfort to Nancy, I put the experience "in the rear-view mirror". We relaxed the remainder of the day and enjoyed a long burning campfire.

DAY #62

Very pleasant temperature this morning as the humidity has decreased. The hot tub and swimming pool fortunately are within walking distance from our site. The club house is sizable and we are pleased to find a pool table. At 11:00 a.m. only two others occupy the pool. This campground must have at least 200 RV's, what are they doing? Not riding horseback! The hot tub erased the memory of yesterday's disappointments, as Nancy was immersed in the pool.

It was necessary to unhook to visit the stables down the steep hillside. Some campers had rented golf carts to "move about" their temporary residence. The young cowgirl was welcoming and unlocked the gate to the ten stall building. Two privately owned horses were the only occupants. When I requested a reservation to ride she checked her list and informed us there were none available for the week. As advertised as a "dude ranch" for 300 camping guests, only four horses is a travesty. Nothing about this resort would motivate me to buy a membership, yet it is filled to near capacity?

DAY #63

We unhooked again today to make the fifteen minute trek to the nearest small town: shopped for groceries and walked through the antique shop. Played pool, Nancy won, and chilled out.

DAY #64

On Saturday mornings the horse arena transfigures to a youngster's rodeo. Probably fifty horse trailers arrive early morning to fetch the participants. Watching those young cowboys and cowgirls celebrate their passion was the highlight of this campground sojourn. Three different age groups competed, first grade, middle school and seniors in high school. Events were widely varied and included steer riding followed by sheep riding. Ninety percent of the high schoolers were female. I have observed that pattern consistently when escorting my young daughter for riding lessons. My developed theory proposes girls reap a psychological "high" when controlling that powerful creature: similar feeling to my reception when in the presence of large boulders.

I received my "horse fix" in spades as a third grade student managed her pet at full speed, hat rebounding from her shoulders, through the obstacles. She raced fearlessly with supreme confidence in her expanded skill. Discovering that passion early in life, bodes well for a healthy future: no need for drugs to get a "high".

Once again we "backed" the football field length to approach our resting place. A longer RV could not "fit" into the slot. It has been our experience that the compact motor home is considerably more utilitarian.

DAY #65

This is the first morning 1 have sensed weariness: ready to move along: been here long enough. When I vocalized my intentions, Nancy emphatically responded "we are staying for the week". I immediately replied in the affirmative. Not often does she rebel to my positioning, and when she does I listen! Game score is Nancy 29 and Jim 28.

DAY #66 & #67

Hot tub, swimming pool, pool table, and walking.

DAY #68

Early morning drive to Pittsburgh, PA to visit my daughter and then onto Cooper Rock State Park near Morgantown, West Virginia. The campground sits atop the mountain overlooking Cheat Lake. Excellent site with plentiful trees and boulders in the background.

DAY #69

Tee time at Lakeview Golf Resort is 10:00 a.m. I taught my son to play the game on this course at age 10. His passion for the sport continues today. At that point in time a non-resident membership was the only club membership I could afford. Our family drove the two hours and my wife and daughter lounged at the large and attractive pool, while my son and I "looked for birdies". As a teenager we played in a father-son tournament and were successful. He hit the long ball and I made putts: that has not changed. However, the course has changed significantly. The layout remained tantalizing, and the course turf management was a contrast. The fairway grass did not exist: actual dry mud, without exaggeration. Without a doubt the most impoverished I have witnessed in my golfing life. I was informed by an employee that the property was recently purchased and is being renovated. The swimming pool was closed and created the impression of a "ghost" structure. The clubhouse, once very becoming with a view of the lake, was sustaining renovation, however in the very early stages. It truly was a shock to my system, following such pleasant memories of my family's numerous years of recreation. I sincerely resent having engaged this reunion: shouldn't expect all experiences to be positive.

Moving south to Kanawha State Forest Campground in Charleston, West Virginia.

DAY #70

The three hour drive after golf yesterday led to our arrival at 6:00 p.m. Plan to utilize the swimming pool, shooting range, and campfire pit today before returning home tomorrow.

DAY #71

Excellent final day of camping yesterday. The capitol building in Charleston is impressive when driving beside the Kanawha River. However, a goodly number of chemical producing towers dominate the landscape. As a young chemist I visited all of those facilities to present my employer's product. Memories are a lifetime treasure. This bucket list adventure will no doubt remain a "top ten".

I am completing this composition on Christmas Day 2024. A great day for celebration!

BUCKET LIST JOURNEY TO AND THRU ALASKA

Departed Franklin, NC ....June 8, 2024

Returned Home............................... August 15, 2024

THE NUMBERS

- ➢ 71 Days of Adventure
- ➢ 43 Driving Days
- ➢ 15,642 Miles
- ➢ 364 Average Miles Per Day
- ➢ $7,244.72 Cost of Gasoline
- ➢ $2,800.56 Cost of Camping
- ➢ $10,045.28 Total Cost of Expedition
- ➢ 23 Excellent Campsites
- ➢ 27 Good Campsites
- ➢ 20 Poor Campsites
- ➢ 5 Viewed Accidents
- ➢ 9 Dangerous Drivers
- ➢ 2 Extended Gridlocks

QUESTIONS AND CONNECTIONS

concernedgrandparents361@gmaiI.com

www.ingramcontent.com/pod-product-compliance
Lightning Source LLC
Chambersburg PA
CBHW041258040426
42334CB00028BA/3076